TRAVELS for BEER

TRAVELS for BEER
By Bill Washawanny

Travel adventures in finding & tasting
great beers and meeting new friends
in distant places.

© Copyright 2007 William J. Washawanny

ISBN 978-0-9796950-0-1

Published 2007
By William J. Washawanny
49 Easton Avenue
New Brunswick, NJ
08901

All rights reserved. No part of this book may be used or reproduced in any manner, without written permission from the author, except in the case of brief quotations embodied in critical articles or reviews.

Thank you!
Dad, for taking the time to proofread the manuscript, even though admitting you are not a beer lover!
and,
Nina, for diligently proofreading the book four times, despite being enticed to reach for a beer each time!

CHEERS!
NA ZDRAVI!
PROST!
SANTE!

To the Boli Crew
of Stuff Yer Face Restaurant
During the first 30 years
1977-2007

Thank you
Dekuji
Danke
Merci

TABLE OF CONTENTS

Introduction
How My Travels for Beer Began 1
Some History You Should Know 5
Plan Your Trip, *but…* 11
The Love for Guinness in Dublin, Ireland 19
Oktoberfest in Munich, Germany 25
Cologne and Dusseldorf, Germany 51
Brussels, Antwerp, and Ghent, Belgium 67
The Pacific Northwest, USA 97
London and Bath, England 117
Bavaria, Germany and Bohemia, Czech Republic 145
Last Call 193

INTRODUCTION

"69 cents a six pack!" yelled out my college roommate. "We can't drink gravel water for that price!" he added. I really didn't know exactly what gravel water was, but I did know that the beer was cheap, cheaper than water. We ordered up about a dozen cases and stashed them away in the hall closet of our beach apartment in Daytona Beach, Florida. We knew they would come in handy, and last us quite awhile. We were wrong about them lasting through a semester, but we did put them to good use.

Those beers in 1973 were always cold, delicious, and drank with the best of friends. I don't remember the brand, maybe Busch or Schlitz, but it just didn't matter. That's what we could afford, that's what we enjoyed together, and that's what started my enjoyment of beer.

I have to admit now, that during the past Holiday season, I purchased a bottle of Samuel Adams Utopias beer, for $125. That's the beer that comes in a replica copper brewing kettle, and set the record for the highest alcohol content of any beer brewed, somewhere around 24%. It tastes more like a fine port, with notes of maple syrup, vanilla and, believe it or not, is fermented in previously used bourbon barrels. It is absolutely delicious.

I'm not sure what my college buddies or I would have thought in the early 70's about the taste of Utopias, or the price of it. We absolutely didn't have the money to spend on it, nor did we have the taste buds to enjoy a beer like Utopias. On the other hand, we did have the camaraderie that would let us enjoy that beer. I can imagine the funny faces and the comments if we had tasted it.

My point is, drink what you like, with people you like, wherever you like. Don't let a beer snob tell you that your taste buds are wacky, or that you're drinking a tasteless beer. On the other hand, there is the old saying "quality over quantity", and there are some spectacular beers in the world, over flowing with great taste. There are thousands of different beers brewed in hundreds of different styles.

This book is about my travel adventures, and spins on my bar stool at home, to locate and taste the great beers of the world. It is a fun collection of observations and stories I have made while learning about the customs and traditions of beer tasting in Europe and America. It is about learning to trust your beer gut feeling and walking down an unmarked alley in an undiscovered city. In the end, you may put on your silly drinking hat and start up a conversation with the beer drinker next to you.

HOW MY TRAVELS FOR BEER BEGAN

I opened a restaurant in New Jersey named Stuff Yer Face, in 1977. It served good quick food, from pretty servers, in a cozy place, near Rutgers University. When I finally got a chance to take some time off, I decided to travel and visit one of my college friends Bill and his wife Barb, in Colorado.

At that time, around 1978, Coors was a cult beer on the East coast. It was not available there, but we had heard of its great taste. We knew Paul Newman drank it after racing his cars, and visitors to Colorado would pack their suitcases with the beer to bring home with them. I knew that I needed to give it a taste. My favorite beer at the time was Moosehead lager from Canada. Moosehead had more flavor than Bud (the King of Beers), or Miller High Life (the champagne of bottled beer). I was also partial to Ballantine ale, because that is what my father usually drank after cutting the lawn on Saturdays, and because they were the sponsors of the New York Yankee televised games. The Ballantine logo included a pretzel, how perfect.

Luckily on my visit to Colorado at this time, I was able to pick up a six of Moosehead. My two friends purchased the Coors. I bragged and bragged that the Moosehead was the best beer that was ever brewed and only a fool could drink anything else. I tasted the Coors, which was pretty darn good. It was very refreshing with that mountain spring water that they boasted about in their ads. However, I couldn't give in to the fact that maybe something was better than Moosehead!

"I'll bet you can't tell the difference between Coors and Moosehead" my friends challenged me. I didn't want to wager on this, but did stick to my guns and still boasted that Moosehead was the best. Somewhere along the trip, they switched beers on me, and poured Coors into my Moosehead bottle. As I drank from the bottle, they of course bust a gut laughing and asking me how much I loved that Moosehead. Okay, so they made a fool out of me, but I did learn a lesson. I did learn that I was passionate about my beer. But why was I so stubborn to taste something new? If you taste something new, you might just like it and find your new favorite.

That night we camped out upstream from the Coors Brewery, and laughed about what happened. We drank plenty of Coors that night, and returned some of that Rocky Mountain spring water to its origin.

Several years later, I was invited to visit the Budweiser brewery in Newark, New Jersey. It was not my first visit to a brewery. My college buddies and I would visit the Bud brewery in Tampa, Florida frequently for the free beer served at the end. I do believe at one point, it was as they say "unlimited" free beer, but then that changed to two free beers, and now it has stopped totally. The visit to Newark in the early 80's was very interesting with one of the Brewmasters giving the talk. We tasted Bud at different stages along its brewing process. Beginning with the taste of the water as it enters the brewery, to the filtered water, to the wort, to the first hopping, and finally the finished beer. It was very informative and interesting.

At one point, the Brewmaster asked us about the tasting notes of the finished Budweiser product we had in our hands. I thought about drinking it on the beach in Daytona during college, and remembered that I always thought the taste had a hint of green apple or citrus in it. I really didn't know what I was talking about, and neither did anyone else around me at that time. But, I mentioned this to the Brewmaster and I was shocked when he said that yes those tasting notes are there! Bud does not add these tastes to the beer, but the special yeast that Anheuser Busch uses to brew the beer gives off those flavors, or esters! Wow, maybe I do know something about beer! Maybe my training has begun to pay off. I pressed my luck a little further by telling the Brewmaster that I also thought Bud in a can was much better than in a bottle...then he told me that I was crazy.

I don't remember when, but I found Pilsner Urquell very early in my drinking years. I must have been looking for something new to taste, and might have been attracted to the marketing package of the green and gold colors and the fancy font that was used. It said something about class, quality, and good taste from old Europe. At the first pop of the bottle cap, the flowery and herbal aromas rose up and caught my nose. Wow, that smells great! The taste was creamy with a little more bitterness from the hops than I was used to, but quite addictive I thought. Urquell was difficult to find, but well worth the search. It remains today as my favorite all round drinking beer. Little did I know that eventually I would make a trip to the city of Pilsen, in the Czech Republic, where it is brewed.

Therefore, looking back, I had built a good foundation for falling in love with beer. By owning my restaurant and getting my first liquor license in 1990, it did afford me the opportunity to add different beers to the menu and to taste them. Tasting them made me curious as to what other beers might be out there in the world of beer and where they were.

I have made over a dozen trips to Europe. The first visit was actually a ski trip to the Alps. However, I found the beer more interesting than the slopes. I found myself returning to Europe almost annually, usually for some specific beer event. Sometimes I traveled alone, sometimes with my brother Tom, or with a friend.

When I met my wife, Nina, and began to travel with her, the adventures took on a higher level of enjoyment. We got married on New Year's Eve 2005, and since then, we have made five journeys to Europe together. Luckily, she likes beer too!

So, our Travels for Beer begins…

Some HISTORY YOU SHOULD KNOW

Beer has an early start in our civilization's history and it is an interesting story. The dates are not exactly important but learning how beer fit into everyday life in the world is.

The first recipe for beer probably didn't get written down for quite some time, because the first time beer was made was most likely by coincidence, or, let's call it good fortune. In the time of the Pharaohs, man had learned to work with different grains and learned to make breads. Likely one day, while making bread outside, it started to rain, and the grains and the rainwater were left to themselves for a time. Wild yeasts, which naturally occur in the air, could have settled on the bread mix. Left alone, the yeast began to eat the sugars in the malted grains, leaving an alcohol-based by-product. The liquid remaining was the first step in making beer. Amazingly, some thirsty soul actually lifted the bowl of liquid to his or her mouth and drank from it. I'm not sure of that first reaction, but we all thank him today for doing that!

Brewing in Germany has a documented beginning in the year 1040. Imagine, that is almost 500 years before Christopher Columbus reached the shores of North America! The Pilgrims who came to America in 1622, also have a beer story to tell. Beer was a supply on the ships. The trip across the ocean took longer than most had planned. The Captain and his crew, wanted to land in an area near Virginia, but had wandered off course to the North, near New England. They could have followed the coastline to make the correction, but the crew was becoming unruly. It seems that the beer supply had run down and was at chronic levels. It's recorded in a shipmate's log that the decision was made to set ashore, set up camp, and hopefully re-establish a beer supply. Now that's a Pilgrim story you don't learn in school. But it points out that beer was a staple of their diet and lives. Have you ever heard the expression "Liquid Bread"? If bread is the staff of life, then so must be beer.

George Washington and Thomas Jefferson were avid brewers. Records of their recipes still exist today. They were farmers, intelligent, and enjoyed food and beverage while entertaining. During the time Washington led the troops during the Revolutionary War he required a ration of beer for each man each day. The Continental Congress paid for it. Good for them, our taxes at work! Thomas Jefferson tried to set up a National Brewery, but it never came to be. William Penn, you know, Mr. Pennsylvania, began the first commercial brewery in 1683.

It's hard to believe that the world drank mostly dark and cloudy beer until 1842. Then a brewer in the city of Pilsen in the Czech Republic delivered the first golden beer. The very first Pilsner beer was Pilsner Urquell. It was truly revolutionary and shocked the world. Afterwards, this style was copied around the world and the golden lager became the most popular brewed and drank beer.

In Europe beer was a staple of their daily life, from children drinking at the table at home, to workers drinking to and from work. It was used for all types of celebrations and special moments. The Germans were great beer drinkers, but, their weekends were family events. The families gathered at park like beer gardens. They would bring their own food. They gathered with neighbors and family members and socialized. There was music, games to play, and there was relaxation. The emphasis of the day was not on the beer, but on the socializing.

It's funny, but beer was at one time considered medicinal and used in hospitals. The famous Guinness stout has advertising posters from the late 1800's with the slogan "Guinness is Good For You".

When the great throngs of immigrants began arriving on the shores of America, they brought with them their favorite beer recipes. Some four million Germans entered our country. Remember the names of Anheuser, Busch, Schlitz, Coors, Pabst, Stroh, Yeungling, Miller, and Leinenkugel? All were German families arriving and starting breweries here in America. Near the turn to the 20th Century there were 1700 breweries in America, beer was big business, and the big brewers were very wealthy men.

Two momentous occasions added to the success of the brewing business, the invention of the bottle cap and the discovery of pasteurization. In the mid 1800's, men and women would walk to the nearest saloon with their own bucket or pail and fill it up with beer to bring home. This beer had a very short shelf life. In 1870, Louis Pasteur found that bacteria were the reason for beer spoiling. He suggested heating the beer to 140 degrees to kill bacteria, a process called pasteurization. Later in 1910, the bottle cap was perfected to keep the beer unaffected by air. These two innovations made fresh beer available to everyone at home. Add in the use of refrigeration at home, and holy cow, the beer was selling!

With the start of World War I in 1914, anti-German sentiment was present in our country and the Temperance movement began an attempt to prohibit the sale of alcohol. These two things spelled trouble for the beer industry and we entered the years of Prohibition. The 18th Amendment to the Constitution was passed in 1920, and for 13 years, alcohol was not legally available in the US. It wasn't until the latter years of the Depression that August Busch, of Anheuser Busch, suggested opening the breweries again to create a million jobs for the jobless and add millions in tax dollars for the government. In 1933, the 21st Amendment was passed and President Roosevelt ended Prohibition.

Beer did however, come under other restrictions during its history besides the United States curtailing manufacturing and sales during the 1920's. The legal drinking age in the US has changed from 21 to 18 and back to 21 again. During the Vietnam War in the early 1970's, the logic was that an 18 year old could vote, go to war, drive a car, or smoke a cigarette, but could not drink a beer.

In England, the Pubs have a closing time of 11pm to help keep the population from drinking excessively. Nevertheless, all that really does is ensure that each person in the bar drinks at a quicker pace near closing time. Restrictions are not the answer to excessive drinking; rather education and familiarity will curtail the abuse. I don't believe that you can legislate morality.

It is hard to understand that beer was at one time considered medicinal, and then at another time, we Americans had thirteen years of Prohibition for the dastardly stuff. It's also hard to believe that the State of Florida, until recently, had archaic laws not allowing the importation of beer in bottles other than 12 or 16 ounces. That means most anything imported from Europe in a 11.2 ounce (1/3 liter) or 16.9 ounce (1/2 liter) bottle was not available. Give me a break! Luckily, that has since changed.

In 1978, President Jimmy Carter showed some legislative initiative. He signed a law enabling small microbreweries to start production again across the nation. Each state could decide their own rules separately, but at least the good beer started to flow again. Today our microbreweries have re-established good tasting, quality, and fresh beer. Once again, there are over one thousand breweries in the USA. These smaller brewers can produce a superior product to the mass produced beers, by giving attention to the details and altering recipes as needed.

While you are sitting on your favorite bar stool drinking your favorite beer trying to figure out all of life's questions, look closely at the bottle's label art. There is a lot of information and history on them to learn. You will notice that some brewers have been in business for hundreds of years. There are catchy, yet educational phrases. There is beautiful artwork. Look at the artwork closely and see things in the background.

So, why is all this history important to you? Respect the history and the challenges that the beer industry has gone through, and you just may enjoy your beer a little bit more. While drinking that next beer, think about traveling to the home country of that beer. It's interesting and a lot of fun! Let's go!

PLAN YOUR TRIP, *but*...

Don't be afraid to walk down that alley. You will notice, as you read along and follow our travels for beer, that Nina and I have developed a beer searching technique. Once we select our destination, we complete some research before our departure to select some special beer locations to find and visit. After arrival, we visit those locations, most likely catch a little buzz, and then move on to something unplanned. Usually we follow our gut feelings and search out something no one else has written about or found yet, sometimes leading us to walk down an unmarked alley. Often, the unplanned stop is the most rewarding.

With today's access to information, world research is so easy. There are periodicals that cover beer in so many ways. From local brew club newsletters, to the weekly food & drink section of your local newspaper, to regional beer newspapers there are reports written on travels to beer destinations. If they seem interesting to you, jot them down and plan to see them yourself.

Examples of regional beer newspapers are *Ale Street News* and *Brewing News*. These papers are terrific. They review the beer news state by state for a particular region of the country, contain informational advertising, and travel reviews. A national beer magazine is *All About Beer*, which comes out six times per year and covers everything you need to know about beer.

Go to the bookstore and read some beer books. Michael Jackson has several in publication that describe his world travels. I own his book, the *Beer Companion*, and in the back is a section titled Hunting the Classic Brews, which lists places where he enjoyed good beer in major cities around the world. If you are good at surfing the web the information is endless. Grab a beer off the shelf of your favorite beer supplier and read the label. It probably has a website listed on it. If not, search the name of the beer or the brewer or the importer and you'll find some kind of information.

My point is, when you travel to a city, have some kind of plan and a select list of beer places to visit. Find them on a map before you leave your home country. Locate your hotel near them. Figure out how to get to them. Make a note of why you are going there. Is it to taste a particular beer? Is it to taste a seasonal specialty of the house? Is it to taste some home made cheese that goes perfectly with the beer?

After your visit to the noted place, then it is time to venture out into the city and find *your* favorite place. Take notice of where the locals are walking. Listen for music in the distant air. Do you smell anything good cooking or brewing? Read the local notices posted on the walls. Look into the windows of shops. Notice the beer advertisements and signs. Maybe if your lucky, you'll see or hear some fine chaps, lads, or mates who are feeling the residuals of a fine establishment. Where did they come from?

I think the first time Nina and I "walked down that alley" to find a great beer place was in Brussels, Belgium. We had already visited some great places that turned up in our research. Beer bars that serve the best, the best way. Falstaff, Cirio, Hotel Metropole, and any of the cafes that are located on Grand Place. Those great Belgian beers served with a stylish goblet to enhance the flavor and aroma of the beer.

When we left our last stop, we started to walk in no particular direction. We round a corner from a very old church, Eglise St. Nicolas, and spot a Corsendonk neon sign about 50 feet down this tiny three foot wide alley. We figure there must be a bar down there. Should we go? At a moment like this, you have to trust your beer gut feeling, your sixth sense.

We opened the door and found "Au Bon Vieux Temps", roughly translated it means "To the Good Old Times". It is small and dark, but offers Westmalle on tap along with other Trappist beers. It has become one of our favorite bars in Brussels, and I will tell you more about it in our Brussels travels. We have been there three times now on two different visits. I have never seen it written up in any tour guide before or since our finding it. Walking down that alley was a great decision that evening.

Another time that Nina and I "walked down that alley" was in Key West, Florida. There is a bridge, 7 Mile Bridge, which connects Marathon Key with Pigeon Key. It is 7 miles long and once a year is closed for an hour and a half for some crazy healthy fools to run a race across it. I've run with my brother Tom about eight times and recently with Nina. Ritual has it that the night of the race we pack up our sneakers and move on South to Key West for the evening.

I like Key West. But, it gets a little boring for a beer guy. Sure, Corona is great to drink during the hot afternoon outside listening to Jimmy Buffet music. When the sun goes down I need something else to drink. There are a couple of local brews to taste from Key West and Miami, which are rather refreshing. Actress Kelly McGillis owns a brew pub in Key West and the Hurricane beers from Miami are good examples. Nina needs something better and so do I. We leave our partying friends at Sloppy Joe's and start wandering the streets. I have been to Key West, more than twenty times in the last twenty years and I am not expecting too much. Nina is thinking more positive.

Quickly we reach a corner of Duval Street and down a quiet side street we see a dimly lit neon sign that seems inviting to the both of us. I don't recognize the joint. Maybe I need to have a few more beers to restore my memory. We walk into a small room, dark, candle lit, with live music and no roof. That's right, no roof. It has walls and a floor but no roof. Okay, it's an outside bar. It just doesn't look like or feel like an outside bar, what with the walls and lights and such. Anyway, we grab a small table for two and wonder what to drink. The music is great, kind of swing like. I approach the bar.

As is typical, there is one bartender working feverishly to serve all the people that have found this off the track place. I scan the beers perched up on the shelf to tell me what they have to offer. Whoa, what's that squat little red bottle with that unusual typeface? It's Chimay Red! Bingo! We've found the goods in Key West. The bartender is impressed that we desire such a beer. She apologizes for not having the proper glass and wishes enjoyment. We found a little bit of beer heaven in the Florida Keys. The music was terrific so we stayed, danced and had a few Chimays. Walking down that alley really paid off for us again.

In the Fall of 2005 Nina and I returned to Europe for the wedding of a couple we had met on New Year's Day of 2005 at the Hofbrauhaus in Munich, Germany. We met Karsten and Heike over nearly eight hours and untold liters of Hofbrauhaus brew, and kept in touch during the year via email. Their wedding was an incredible eighteen-hour marathon. Two days later, the bride and groom took us on a little tour of their area, Schwabisch Hall, Germany. The Schwabisch area is known for a famous black pig, which also happens to have a beer named after it. The tour included Rothenburg, reminiscent of a Christmas village, and the bride's family farm. A highlight of the farm was the grandfather's distillery where he produced schnaps using the fruit he grew on the farm. It was an exciting moment to be in his licensed distillery, which was only a small section of the basement. Cheerfully, we were given small bottles of the schnaps to take home as souvenirs.

After leaving Karsten and Heike, one of our stops was in Regensberg, Germany. A University city, that was very Medieval with narrow twisting streets, and a few great local breweries. We walked the streets during the day sampling beers from the local breweries.

In the evening after an Italian dinner, we just started to wander the cobblestone streets. We had no particular destination in mind. We had already been to the places that we had researched, however, we could use one more beer before the end of the night. When you walk a city all day, sometimes you seem to run out of different streets to walk down. I think we were both feeling this way at this point.

Just when we really need that new turn, we see a neon sign brightly lit down an alley. An alley that was even less narrow than most of the local streets. This place has our names all over it! We walk in, and there is a young woman behind the bar. She gives us a nice smile, but she is obviously cleaning up for the end of the night. She tells us so, but offers us a drink while she is closing up. We ask for something local and drink a Weltenburger bock. Both Nina and I are amazed at how delicious this bitter sweet chocolate beer is, and make a note in our log. We strike up a conversation with Charme, who struggles with her English.

I explain to her that I own a bar in the US and know what it is like to clean up and have customers hanging around. She seems to relax and has a beer with us. Her work slows. We tell her about our experiences at the Schwabisch wedding and the invite to the family farm and how the grandfather makes schnaps. Before we know it, with a big smile, she grabs a bottle of schnaps from underneath the bar and offers us a sip. She explains that her Oma, or grandmother, makes it at home! We laughed so hard. We raised our glasses, all of us said prost, and new friends were made. Nina and I were glad that Charme kept the neon light shining bright, down her alley, while closing.

Philadelphia is another great beer city. In the Old Historic District, the streets are narrow and remind me of Europe's old towns. It is amazing how you can wander the pubs of Philadelphia and walk out a door that is within shouting distance of the Liberty Bell or Independence Hall. It's a great beer city because you can visit the pubs almost classified by country. There are Irish pubs, German pubs, and Belgian pubs, etc. There are pubs in Philly, which feature just the local brews and are proud of them.

Nina and I went to Philly in the Fall of 2004 for a couple of nights. I was familiar with the lay of the town and where the famous pubs were. It was a cool evening, clear air, and most of the leaves from the trees were laying on the ground. We had just finished a session at McGillin's Olde Ale House. McGillin's has been around for 140 years! I have always used the front door, but we notice some people coming and going from a side door. We decide to exit that way and see where it takes us.

It takes us to an alley of course. It might be one of those 18th Century streets of the Historic District. It's now a little foggy, and in the distance we hear what we think are bag pipes playing. We quicken the pace and try to follow the fog piercing sounds. We round the corner and the music gets louder. We soon see the bag pipers, a group of four or five, exiting a pub and heading down the street. We decide to follow.

They don't have to walk too far before they find and enter another pub. The crowded bar makes room for the boys and they gladly continue to play. This was great stuff. The crowd in the bar stops its conversations and listens to the band. They play a couple of patriotic songs and make an announcement. The band has been traveling around the US and now is trying to raise some money for their trip home to Scotland. The hat is passed and some free beers given away. All in all, it was a very nostalgic night in this alley in the City of Independence.

So, before you travel, make a list of pubs you must visit at your destination of choice. Nina and I have been very lucky with our pub searches. The pubs on our list of "must see" always prove to be worthy of their reputation. But, the pubs that we find down the alleys, not on any list, are worth the risk and sometimes become our favorite or most memorable place.

THE LOVE FOR GUINNESS IN DUBLIN, IRELAND

Ireland, the Emerald Island, and Dublin should be on any beer drinkers' list of places to visit. We have all heard the great stories of the pubs, St. Patrick's Day, friendly people, and the great stout beers. Dublin is the capital of Ireland, located on the East coast of the island. The River Leffey flows through the capital and supplies the water to make the Guinness.

Arthur Guinness bought a run down brewery at St. James Gate in 1759. He signed a 9000 year lease with free water included. Now that's a deal not even Trump could top! In 1799 he decided to focus on brewing the new stout style and wrote "Ours is the work of genius. I have made my mark." Well, that he did. Guinness stout is sold around the world in many variations. The Brewery at St. James remains and it is a tourist destination that should not be missed, at least to get the two free pints at the end of the tour.

We are all familiar with Guinness stout draught. It is a great dark beer from Ireland. It tastes of caramel at first, then becomes somewhat dry, a little sweet, and has hints of roasted coffee. A special mix of nitrogen and carbon dioxide is used in the draft system. The beer is always served with that famous volcanic eruption going on in the glass with the pretty cream colored head. The bubbles rise and sink within the glass. Some people think of it as a real heavy beer, high in alcohol and usually served warm.

Americans might be right, in thinking that way, because Guinness sometimes gets no respect here in the States. Guinness goes to great lengths to teach how to properly store and serve its product. It even issues certificates to establishments that serve the "Perfect Pint" when the Guinness Police show up for a spot check. When it is poured correctly, it is one of the classic and favorite beers of the world. It is not a heavy beer, but rather light. It is not high in alcohol, but about average at 4.1%. It should not be served warm, but at a nice cool recommended temperature of 45 degrees.

I was first swayed by its allurement by tasting the Black and Tan drink. A Black and Tan is half English Bass ale and half Irish Guinness stout. The Guinness is lighter than the Bass and is the upper floating half of the solution. Usually when you drink it, the Bass slips out from under the Guinness and enters your mouth first. I had already known about the slightly malty taste of the Bass. But, as you proceed to drink, the two kind of mix and I learned about the great taste of Guinness. After the first Black and Tan, I began to order only the Guinness.

When I made my first trip to Dublin I had a friend of a friend of my brother who owned a pub, named O'Looney's. Yes, the perfect name for a pub, but it really was their last name. I had never met Brian O'Looney but they had met my brother in Florida. As I entered into the pub and walked from the door to the bar, the bartender yelled out to me, "You must be Tom's brother!" I couldn't believe that he could recognize me that quickly without having ever met me. Moreover, while working!

From the second I walked in, I was welcomed and treated like a regular. Two cousins were sitting at the bar next to me and they kept the conversation flowing. The Guinness was also flowing. I went on a tour of the pub, including a visit to the basement and the beer cooler. Since I was also a bar owner, I was very interested in seeing the workings of the Guinness pub. I was very impressed, and surprised, to find that they were not using any tanks of gas for pushing the beer upstairs. They had a unit mounted on an outside wall that converted the outside air into a useable gas mixture to push the Guinness. *Brilliant!*

Back upstairs, I was given a lesson on how to properly pour a pint of Guinness. Where to aim the first shot into the glass, the perfect angle of the glass, how thick should the foam be at the top. It all takes time, and is actually a two or three step process. They are very precise about this. It must have taken three or four tries to get it right. But, there was no waste of the Guinness! I had a great visit that evening and eventually stayed after hours. I felt just like a regular here.

The conversation at the bars of Dublin flows as smoothly as the Guinness. Lively people they are, listening and chatting, and drinking, and not watching any TV or playing any video games. They are there for the conversation, and of course, the Guinness. It's called "kraik" in Ireland, the good times at the pub.

They truly believe in their Guinness. Years ago they believed that Guinness had medicinal properties and was good for you. It was actually served in hospitals before the turn of the 20th Century. Guinness has many artful posters from their past and it is clearly advertised that way. "Guinness is Good for You!" "Guinness Gives You Strength!"

Someone sitting at the bar with me at one of the pubs in town knew that I was an American by the way I drank from my pint. He noticed that there were many small rings of foam left inside my glass. This indicated that I took many small sips of the beer. He stated that the Europeans drank in a way that left fewer rings of foam, indicating less sips, but longer sips. I considered the facts and realized he was correct. Americans seem to rush through the beer with a sip, sip, sip and a little talking. On the other hand I noticed in

Dublin that most people were talking, talking, talking and taking a large, long sip.

In the pubs in Dublin you will notice that there are half filled pints sitting on the top of the bar near the taps. Don't reach for any of those! These pints are only getting ready. They are just half way through the proper process. They will be topped off with more Guinness for a second time and maybe a third before perfection. If you are in a rush, don't be, perfection takes time. Don't ask for your Guinness a second time either, they get a little angry about it. One last thing, don't drink your pint the second you receive it, wait a half a minute for the volcanic eruption to settle down inside the glass, you may get some funny looks, but it will start a conversation.

As I drank my Guinness at O'Looney's, I commented how much more delicious the Guinness tasted here in Dublin than in the States. We all understood that the beer had to travel across the ocean to get there and how could anything survive intact after that? True, the heat and time had something to do with it. They suggested that I have a Guinness at a pub that is closer to the St. Jame's Gate Brewery, where the Guinness would be even fresher and tastier! Okay, enough is enough. Do you really think the Guinness would be tastier and fresher closer to the brewery? Yes, I believe that they did. I, of course, did eventually find a pub closer and I did take the brewery tour at St. James Gate. I received my two free pints at the end of tour, and guess what? Those were the tastiest two pints of Guinness I had ever had.

If you are drinking Guinness in the USA, look on the walls for a "Perfect Pint" certificate, it may indicate that you will get the best we can offer. Hopefully, your bartender won't rush you a one pour Guinness.

I have also noticed in the USA and in Europe that on a large percentage of the menus, Guinness is spelled with only one 'N'. I don't mean just once in a while, but most of the time! Now that shows you that maybe that pub is not giving it the attention and respect it deserves. Check it out the next pub you visit.

I hope to return to Ireland soon. My trip was only for three nights in Dublin. I can envision a ten-day tour around the island visiting as many pubs as possible.

SLAINTE!

OKTOBERFEST IN MUNICH, GERMANY

So, Prince Ludwig marries Princess Therese in 1810 with a grand celebration that lasts a week. They dance, drink beer, hunt, and carry on. Little did they know that people from around the world would still be helping them celebrate some 200 years later. The Grand Daddy of all beer festivals where over six million liters of beer are drank and umpteen pounds of sausage are eaten each year during a 16-day period held on the festival grounds known as the Theresienwiese or just "die Wiesn".

Munich is the capital of Bavaria, located in the South East area of Germany. Bavaria is known for its great lagers and weisse beers, and Bavarians are known for their drinking skills.

If you like beer and enjoy traveling, a visit to this party called Oktoberfest is necessary. Do not be scared. Do some planning, book your flights and rooms early and just go. You will never forget it. You will tell the stories for the rest of your life. There is some information to know before you arrive and some information you will learn while you are there. I will tell you some now, but you will just have to learn some of it on your own by experience.

Oktoberfest normally ends on the first Sunday of October, and begins two weekends earlier on a Saturday morning. Book your rooms early if you care about such things as a private bathroom, clean sheets, and close proximaty. Rooms in Munich within walking distance to the fest grounds fill up almost a year in advance. Do not even think about driving to the festival! Walking is best. Even if it's not in a straight line! Mass transit is very convenient.

My first visit was in 1992 with my brother Tom. I was 38 years old. We combined the trip with visits to Nurnberg, Prague, and Salzburg. I think Munich was the last stop of our trip. It may be better if you start there, because you will need your strength. You may consider the days in the other cities before Munich as practice, but really, it is too late to practice now. This is the real thing, the big game. You're either ready now, or you're not.

After checking in at our hotel on a late Thursday morning, we decided to immediately go to the festival and check it out. We did not know exactly where it was, but had a good idea in which direction to head. Once on our way, we noticed we were in an electrical wave of people heading in the same direction, somewhere. The pace was quick and the chatter was gleeful. I spotted a street sign that read "Festwiese" with a straight-ahead arrow. That was it! Around the corner from St. Mark's Church is the festival's entrance. Thousands of people, wide street ways, and ornate "beer tents" appeared ahead of us.

When you read about beer tents, you will not envision what it really is like. These tents stand probably 30 feet tall, hold about 10,000 partiers, a band in the center, countless toilets (pissorts), multiple kitchens, gift stands, and huge mug washing stations. The sponsoring beer company ornately decorates each tent. Unbelievably, after each year's festival, the tents are taken down and re-built during the next summer.

Remember, that only the six Munich brewers can sponsor a tent, that's Spaten, Lowenbrau, Paulaner, Augustiner, Hofbrau, and Hacker Pschor. It was just after lunchtime for our first visit, and easy to get a seat at the large tables. The tent was nearly ¾ full. Just as you picture it, a large buxom woman brings us our first mugs of "helles" or light gold beer, in liter mugs. We laugh, we toast, we drink and we're off! Delicious. The band is playing German songs and, to our surprise, old American favorites like Frank Sinatra and John Denver. We decide to take precautions and after our second liter order some food. We recognize the words for chicken on the menu and order that. What arrived was a half roasted chicken with tasty spices and mashed potatoes. It is the perfect meal for drinking mass quantities of beer.

It seems that every ten minutes or so, the band plays a song "Ein Prosit". It's a simple song, about four lines long, and everyone knows the words. The song is simply a group cheers to the good times. The crowd sings along, raises their mugs, toasts their table companions and takes a good swig on the count of three. "PROST!" The band really does take charge of the crowd and sets the pace of the party. There is a German word, "gemutlichkeit", which roughly translates to, good times. Comparable to the Irish "kraik", the atmosphere or fun being had in the pub.

Very quickly, you find yourself making conversation with everyone around you. By this time for us, our table companions were three female students from the West Coast of the USA. They too were enjoying the beer and the atmosphere. We drank and talked with them all afternoon, having a grand old time. Then about 4:30, the waitress placed a reservation sign on our table for 5pm! Don't sit at a table with a reserved sign on it, even if the reservation is not for hours later. The tent is nearing capacity with new arrivals from the local workforce. We are about to lose our seats. Where are we going to go? We're not done partying yet. Five liters is just not enough for the first day.

The girls make eyes with some Italian guys a couple of tables over. One by one they slip away from us to the safety of a non-reserved table. But, true to beer drinkers across the globe, our bond was secure. The girls cleared the way for us to join them, with the approval of the Italians. The Italians even came ready with there own picnic of cheese and sausage. The beer continued to flow, the band continued to play, the clanging of mugs was heard everywhere. Conversation was continually about nothing, but also about everything. There was sign language, hand gesturing, eyebrow raising, body language, and translations being done by three or four people in as many languages to get a story told. No one is ever sure that their story is understood by everyone, but at the end of the story, if the mugs are raised, and everyone yells Prost, then it just doesn't matter.

I'm not sure how many liters were drank that day and evening, but we did find ourselves safely in our own beds the next morning. I remember leaving the tent and seeing the famous "hill". Behind some of the tents on the Western side of the fest grounds there is a small hill, which will eventually fill up with people laying down and taking a little snooze. Nobody bothers them, they are just resting up for their second round. I also noticed that night that in some of the toilet areas there are vomitoriums. No kidding. It is a large sink with a large faucet mounted on a hose to clean up yourself and the sink.

We didn't visit the Fest on that Friday. We used the day for a little sightseeing within Munich. There are many biergartens and brauhauses in the city. Any of them are just perfect to visit. From the Augustiner biegarten under the chestnut trees, to the world famous Hofbrauhaus, both of these have seating capacities of over 10,000 each! Centrally located on the Marienplatz is Augustiner's Brauhaus and the Spaten Hof is right next door. Great food and the same tasty beers are available at each, along with the famous band and the gemutlichkeite. Just remember, do not sit a table that has a sign hanging over it or on it that says "Stammtisch". This table is strictly reserved for the locals. You will be asked to leave. However, it could be your goal to get an invite to sit at the Stammtisch!

Saturday we were in good shape to experience the last Saturday night of that year's festival. We arrived late in the afternoon and decided to walk around and see what else was on the grounds. There are lots of amusement rides for the kids and adults, games of chance, ice cream, giant delicious pretzels, roasting pig and ox knuckles, and smoked fish on a stick! While walking behind one of the tents looking for a pissort, I was abruptly pushed aside by a fellow in a security uniform, blowing a whistle, and yelling some unintelligible words. But, the picture was perfect! Directly in front of me a beer wagon drawn by a team of horses had just pulled up and they were delivering wooden kegs of beer! The security team was pushing people aside to clear a path for the kegs to be rolled into the beer tent. Wow, it was the best use of security that I had ever seen in my life. What priorities!

The sight of that beer being rolled into the tent, just made me thirsty and it was time for Tom and I to enter the tent and get a beer. We started with the Augustiner tent because some of the locals had told us that it was the best local beer. We approached the double doors of the main entrance of the Augustiner tent and were met by a mean security guard and a notice, hand written, noting that the tent was filled to capacity! What? It's closed? We can't get a beer? Well there must be something special going on here, so we move on to the Spaten tent. Same experience, closed! Uh-oh, we are in trouble. We're at the last Saturday of the 1992 Oktoberfest 3500 miles from home and we can't get a beer?

Being from New Jersey, we are not shut out that easy. We walk around to the side entrance near the kitchens and easily slip inside and into a mass of people standing on benches, arms and mugs raised above their heads all singing together and toasting new friends. The band was playing "Ein Prosit". The feeling of the force of these people was quite overwhelming and intimidating. How are we going to find a place to sit in this crowd? There was barely room in the large aisle ways to walk around. Constantly we saw beer girls walking by with armfuls of liter mugs filled with golden liquid and topped off in white foam. Half of the people were wearing funny drinking hats. There were keg hats, mug hats, pig hats and hillbilly hats. We saw people climbing on the benches around other people to head to the pissorts. We're too late! We can't catch up now. We'll never get a beer.

I flag down one of the girls and try to purchase two beers. I was informed of a rule we hadn't learned our first visit on that quiet afternoon. You must have a seat to order and receive a beer. No way. We are not going to get a seat or a beer here tonight. The crowd is thirsty and they are getting thirstier with all the prosting and singing. So, did I mention that we are from New Jersey? What are we to do? Of course, let's bribe the beer girls! We offer double the money for a liter, quite a good tip for her. She agrees and tells us to lean against a garbage can that is in the aisle, so that she can find us when she returns. What seems like a hundred years, surrounded by people who seem to have been partying since the night before last, we stand dry mouthed waiting to see if our new best friend really returns with the beer. She does! As is typical, the mugs are a little warm from the dishwasher and only about ¾ full below the liter mark, but filled with cold golden beer! Finally we feel like we have cracked the code and are part of this massive population, we do belong.

Our friendly and now wealthy Beer Goddess returns a couple of more times with great mugs of helles, light golden lager. We never walk away from our garbage can in the aisle, which also rests at the end of a table with a family of locals enjoying their table reservation. I notice that they seem to be angry at us. I feel a little bad, but how else can we get a beer without a little bribery? I make eye contact with a woman, raise my mug, and offer her a Prost! She returns a warm smile with her Prost, and gets up from her bench and makes her way over to me.

It seems she is not mad at us for bribing the beer girl or standing in the aisle drinking our beers, but she is angry that we have to pay that much money. She and her family offer to order our beers for us from their table and then we would only have to pay the regular price. It just wasn't fair she thought. We agreed. She apologized for not being able to squeeze us in at their table, but it really was just impossible, and they had more family arriving every minute.

At one point, Tom and I had to offer up some of our space around our garbage can to members of their family who didn't have a seat either. It seems most Germans enjoy practicing their English and love to chat. We spent the entire night with them, at the garbage can, and even got a golf invite for the next morning. Sorry, no thanks, no golf for me tomorrow.

I didn't return to the festival the next day, Sunday. My stomach didn't seem to like the famous radish snack they serve up. They grow giant radishes and spiral cut them in a way that they are still connected, almost snake like. Several of these radishes are served on a plate, salted, and they really taste great with the beer. That was the end of the '92 Fest. We had a great time, and knew we would return someday.

I believe it was three years later when Tom and I returned to Munich for another go at it. This time I did some research and had a plan. Learn some German language before arriving. It helps with making friendly with the locals and a little bit goes a long way. "Ist desser platz bezets?" means are these seats taken in Deutsch. I am always surprised at the fact that even though the local residents say they only speak a little English, they can carry on a conversation with you for four hours over some beers. The beer servers will appreciate that you try to speak the local language and they will be friendlier to you, and probably switch to English anyway.

On the internet web site for the Munich tourist board you can find some great information on the festival. The website lists the phone numbers for the various tents you can contact to make table reservations. There are tourist agencies that will book your hotel rooms along with a one night table reservation at the festival. That could come in handy for the bashful. This visit I was going to try my German to find a seat, or visit the Hippodrome tent. The Hippodrome tent is sponsored by the Hofbrauhaus and might be one of the more loud and festive tents, but they actually have some American like high top bar tables where you can lean, order and drink a beer. My brother and I gave this a shot. (no pun intended, but there are small schnaps stands spread out through the wiesen).

The crowd is a little rougher here, mostly male. It's okay to start this way, but I wouldn't want to finish my session here. The first guy I met was asking me if I wanted a hit off of his smoke. Didn't look like a cigarette. I asked him about it and he said he just rolled it using the fresh hops in the tent used as decorations. Well that's a clever idea. No thanks I'll drink my hops, not smoke it. He seemed to be enjoying himself. There was a group of guys stacking their empty liter mugs in a pyramid. I was surprised they could get away with that. But then again it was the Hippodrome. Shortly, the band stopped playing and the bandleader was making an announcement.

I am not sure what he said, but an elderly lady walked up onto the stage, gingerly carrying her liter of beer. She seemed to be some important local person, maybe involved with the Hofbrauhaus or maybe celebrating her 90th

birthday. Expecting a speech or a toast, I was shocked when the music kicked up and she threw her liter back and proceeded to chug the entire thing in less than a minute! The crowd was impressed and showed their appreciation (and respect) by hoisting their own mugs up in the air and yelling Prost! By the time we finished laughing about that, and ordering our own next round, guess who walks out on the stage? Here she is again, liter in hand, the band is ready, and there goes the beer just as quick as the last time. Unbelievable. I think she repeated this three or four times during the evening. I have to admit though, that over the years, the speed and frequency of the beers disappearing has grown.

The next day we went in the early part of the afternoon, which is a little quieter than the evenings. We quickly found some seats at a table where a young German couple was enjoying beer. It's not easy sitting across from strangers at a table, but as soon as the beer comes, give a loud Prost and a smile. I'm 100% sure that a Prost will be returned with a smile and the fun begins. Conversation is really why everyone is there. The beer isn't that good or that cold. But meeting the different people is the fun of it. International friends can be made so easily.

I remember the names of the couple, Klaus and Monica. (And I don't remember what I had for dinner last night.) He worked in an auto service center and she was a teacher, together they had two girls. They spoke very little English and we spoke very little German, but we got along. What really helped us was the English/Deutsch dictionary that I brought out on the table. The dictionary really got the conversation moving and they bought the first shared round of beers. We bought a pretzel to share and we laughed and had some serious talks. We even discussed the reunification of East and West Germany, which had just recently happened.

Soon their young girls took a break from the amusement rides and stopped at our table. Of course children of that age learn languages quickly and easily, and helped with the translations. To my surprise, they shared a dark beer. I had thought that the dark beer was no longer served at Oktoberfest and only the light or helles was available. It must have been the last year that it was served. It was a pleasant afternoon session but I was really feeling the beers. Monica and Klaus said good bye and Tom and I were left at the table with two open seats. Immediately, two young males occupy the seats.

Now I have neglected to state that the woman serving the beers to our table was just postcard beautiful. She had long blonde hair matching the golden color of the beer and fitting perfectly in her traditional dress, the dirndle. The two new tablemates laughed when she approached and they received kisses of hello. We quickly found out that she is the sister of one of them. Now isn't that just our luck? Just about 3 sheets to the wind and Tom and I are about to get introduced to a beautiful beer maiden. Well, wisdom prevailed and one liter later, I had to call it a day. The words just weren't coming out right, not the English words nor the German words.

This might be a good time to explain the bathrooms designed for the men, or Herren. Now picture 100,000 people, a large percentage male, with no real purpose for the day or night except to drink beer and be merry. Somebody has got to take a piss. (Or is it give a piss?) The Germans, in all their efficiency, have placed around the massive tents, pissorts. These pissorts vary in size, but picture a room about 12′ x 20′ with a waterfall continually running down each of the stainless steel walls. At the base of each wall is a trough with a gently flowing river of water in it. It is quite amazing how fast and how many guys that can pass through that room. Wear old shoes. If you use two hands to do your business, keep your wallet tightly tucked away.

The next visit was in 1998. I did a little research again before booking and found that there was a parade the morning of the first Saturday. Now this I had to see. Everyone loves a parade. A beer parade? Again, brother Tom was up for the trip. We arrive in Munich on a Friday. We wander out to the city's main square, the Marienplatz, and quickly find ourselves in the Hofbrauhaus. The Hofbrauhaus is about 400 years old, has a seating capacity of over 10,000, serves great food, and has a band that looks like they have been there since opening day, and they sound great. Tom and I have a couple of beers and dinner in the biergarten and drag each other home early so we can be fresh for the BIG day. The parade starts at 10am, we figure at least an hour or two early to get a good spot. We didn't really know what to expect but it had to be good, right?

Tom and I had gone to President Reagan's first Innauguration in 1980. It was a blustery, awful cold day in January. We stood on the side of the street for four hours, huddled and pressed together with the crowd. We got to see the president's limo for a few quick seconds. This parade should be just a tad better.

The morning was perfect with a clear blue sky, 60 degrees, it was good biergarten drinking weather. The plan was for the parade to run about 1½ hours from the city center about two miles to the fest grounds, the Wiesen. The first keg of beer is traditionally tapped in the Spaten beer tent at noon by the Lord Mayor of Munchen and is marked by a blast from a cannon. Spaten gets the honor because their brewers were the first to brew the golden elixir. With the words "o' zapft itz", meaning "it's tapped!", the wooden keg begins to flow its liquid gold.

The parade was terrific. Traditional horse drawn wooden carriages ferry dignitaries and beer. The horses are dressed up for the day with bells and colorful strappings. The townspeople display their traditional clothing. Marching bands from different areas of the region, hops growers, brewers and more beer are on parade. Some of the wagons have members of staff on board singing, and of course drinking the beer. If your lucky, the wagon will stop in front of you and if offered, you could partake in a little shared beer before the official opening. It's impressive to me the pride that is taken in their industry of beer making and the eye towards tradition. It makes you want to cry, but even more it makes you want to drink a beer!

When the last wagon passes, we follow on foot into the fest grounds. Slowly we walk en masse (en mass also means large beer). We hear the cannon blast and everyone cheers, we know that the first keg has been tapped. Inch by inch we follow the crowd first past the Hippodrome tent, then the Spaten tent. We avoid each, remembering past experiences at the Hippo, and that the Spaten tent would be too crowded because of the opening festivities. We enter the Paulaner tent and are immediately knee deep in drunken bastards. These people skipped the parade and must have been here since sun up! I guess I was wrong about that tradition stuff.

Getting a seat was really tough. But, being the professionals that we are now, we grabbed two seats outside on that beautiful day. We had perfect seats for watching the huge blue and white Paulaner mug sign slowly spin overhead. I knew that would be a sign of what was ahead for us; lots of Paulaner and lots of spinning. Our biergarten was along side of the Paulaner main tent, with a small street behind us. The street was busy with remnants from the parade. Horses and beer wagons were going by, marching bands, and constant beer deliveries. It made for a very enjoyable afternoon.

I am always amazed at how efficient the service is at Oktoberfest. So many people, yet you get your beer and food without much of a wait. The people share their food, but not their beer. They will raise their mugs to you and give you a cheer. At our outside seats we met a couple from Texas. They seemed a little overwhelmed by the whole thing but were able to toss back a couple of liters. I tested out my new mini video cam and promised them I would send them a copy of the tape. When I returned to the States I did send the tape, but I was surprised that I never received an acknowledgment of receipt. That just doesn't fit in with the spirit and camaraderie of Oktoberfest.

During this visit to Oktoberfest I noticed for the first time, the statue erected in honor of Princess Therese and Bavaria. It reminds me of the Statue of Liberty, not nearly as tall but standing about 200 feet, it occupies a space in the rear of the grounds. It was erected in 1850. You can climb in the statue and at the top, you get a great vantage point to view the grounds.

I returned again in 2002, this time by myself, equipped with coupons and passes given to me by our Spaten distributor in the US. It seems that Stuff Yer Face is a top seller of Franziskaner Weisse beer in New Jersey. Franziskaner Brewing is now owned by Spaten. Free food, free beer, but no table reservations. I also have a friend from New Jersey who had been dating a local German both of which will be in Munich during my visit. Jurgen and Heidi live locally in Munich and I gave them a call. They express their eagerness to meet me at the festival, but Jurgen being in his 60's, has opted to go early about 11am and not to over do it. We'll visit the more quiet and smaller tent, the Kaifer's Wieesen Schanke. This tent was perfect for me. We will be away from the real rowdies, very much in the local flavor. I had met Jurgen before in NJ, and found out that he bears the title of Count. Count of what I don't know, but he was an affable gent.

We met at the pre-determined time of 11am and ordered our first liter. Conversation was easy, the weather was perfect, almost too warm nearing 85 degrees. As usual in the Oktoberfest tents, the atmosphere takes over. The music plays, the smiles brim, the beer is poured, and the laughter gets louder. I'm glad Jurgen wanted to start early and end early, and take it easy. After five liters we finally called it quits, and headed out of the fest grounds to get dinner.

My next return to Munich and Oktoberfest was in 2005 with Nina, my wife to be in just a few months. Nina is the type of girl whose smile brightens up the room and her engaging conversation makes friends anywhere. She is the perfect person to visit Europe with, and she too likes to taste and drink different beers. This visit we come equipped with coupons from Spaten and most importantly, table reservations! Yes, it has finally happened, we have seat reservations for a Friday evening at 5pm in the Lowenbrau tent. Thank you to all my customers at Stuff Yer Face for purchasing and drinking Franziskaner and making Stuff Yer Face the number one account for Northern New Jersey.

This reservation stuff is perfect timing for me. I'm older now, 51, engaged to be married, and traveling with my bride to be. I'm not ready for that knock down drinking on the main floor of the beer tents. We arrive at 4:30 and flash our printed reservation. It is acknowledged and we are escorted up to a mezzanine level of the tent. We are feeling very important. It is a little hot and smoky. Jackets and sweatshirts are hanging from the rafters of the tent. The band is playing and of course, most everyone has been enjoying the beer since 11am. To our surprise a few Americans, who are working and living in Germany, quickly greet us. They noticed the table reservation for Stuff

Yer Face during the afternoon and couldn't wait to meet us and say hi. So it began, even without our first beers.

Waiting for those first beers is excruciating. We miss the first toast while the band plays "Ein Prosit", and we patiently watch everyone having the time of their lives. Finally, they arrive, and Nina and I toast each other. People offer to take our first photo. It was easy this time, we are in, and let the festivities begin. Nina quickly gets in step with the crowd and meets everyone around us. Has she been here before? No, just natural abilities. She has a table of teenagers flirting with her, and a group of experienced locals getting jealous also.

Soon we notice that someone of notoriety has arrived a couple of tables away. She looks like a beauty pageant winner with her sash worn across her chest. We get a glimpse of it and it reads "Hops Princess" of Tettnanger. I go over to introduce myself to the Hops Princess and learn her name is Sandra. She speaks English well enough, is cute, and is as expected, well informed on the hops used in brewing the beer. She also likes to drink the beer, so we carry on a conversation and she moves over to where Nina and I are sitting. It seems she is there for hours, drinking, conversing, and signing postcards for her fans. Towards the end of the evening, another hops Princess and her majesty, the Queen of Hops, join us at our table.

We party with a large group from Japan sharing silly hats and photos. There were new giant foam hats this year. We select one in pink for Nina with the face of girly pig on it, and another for me with lederhosen on it. We share conversation and laughing with a group of local elderly gents. We share laughing and pin exchanges with a group of young local lads. Jurgen from Landshut, Germany, and his friend Nicole translate all of this for us. We met them very early on in the evening. Our table had a few vacant seats and they approached and asked if they were open. At first they were slightly reluctant to speak with us. But as usual, after the first beer and a Prost and a smile we broke down the barriers and a conversation begins. Jurgen and Nicole are technically our guests at our table because they did not have a reservation.

It seems ironic that Nina and I from America, are hosting two locals at their national festival. Jurgen spoke English very well, and was more than enthusiastic about translanting all that was being said around us that we didn't quite understand. I returned the favor by being his escort to and from the pissort. Remember, he and Nicole had no passes to get back into the reserved section after leaving the seats. So each time Jurgen had to piss, I had to escort him to and from the reserved seats through the security. It was my pleasure, I had earned my seats by being to Oktoberfest for a fifth time.

The night soon comes to an end. Suddenly someone walks behind me and taps me on the shoulder. I turn around. An elderly man speaking English, in a thick German accent, tells me to thank my father and other fathers from America for coming in World War II, for without them this festival could never happen. Just as quickly as he approached, he leaves. I can say nothing, and pause for a moment to think of my father who did serve during the war. I think words of thanks to myself.

I never really remember leaving the tent on any of my visits, just arriving. The Hops Royalty invites us out for a party at someone's house after the fest ends. Nina and I would love to, but how much is enough? If the party was close, maybe yes, but we were informed that train travel was needed. So reluctantly, we declined. We had made enough memories and friends for one night. We climbed up on the bench one more time, grabbed our sweatshirts, wore our new fest hats high, and bid everyone an "auf wiedersehn".

I'm so glad that I was able to attend an Oktoberfest with Nina and Tom. It is hard to describe the festivities to someone who has not attended. We now have the stories and the feelings to share. The beer is not the reason to go. Sure, the beer is the great socializer and breaks down the social barriers, but the reason is the resulting bonds and camaraderie of the people participating. It seems such a simple thought, but if only the leaders of the world could once in a while sit across from one another at a table, wear a silly looking hat, listen to some cheerful music and drink a large beer, could they then have a chance to understand each other and not see each other as an enemy. When you wear a silly hat, it seems everyone is equal, and looking to just enjoy life.

I have no plans to return to Oktoberfest. I was one of the six million each year that attend, five times. I have learned my lessons well, and can use them anywhere and teach them to anyone who is willing to learn and listen. Munchen is a beautiful city and now one of my favorites. You can visit Munchen anytime other than Oktoberfest and still experience the excitement of the biergarten or bierhall within the city. I can play the CD's that I have and pick up a six pack of Oktoberfest beer anytime I want at home and get the photo album out. If you can't make it to Germany, local Octoberfest parties are held almost anywhere during the months of September and October. Put your silly hat on your head and go!

PROST!

KLOSTER ANDECHS

A great day trip while staying in Munich is to visit Kloster Andechs. As if there aren't enough places to drink great beer within Munich. The Kloster lies south of Munich, about 30 minutes travel time via the S-Bahn #5. The last stop is Herrshing, where you can catch a local bus operated by Rauner for a ten-minute ride to the Monastery. Or, you can walk from the train station to the Monastery on some forest trails in about an hour.

The Benedictine Monastery lies atop Holy Mountain, located on the eastern side of Lake Ammersee. The scenery and view are great from the top. On the site are several braustuberls, the klostergasthof, church, meeting halls and beer gardens. The actual brewery is located at the foot of the mountain and is modernized regularly to meet the demand.

If you go, the beer and the food are only sold from 10 am to 8 pm, in respect for the monks' life of silence. Nina and I are planning to visit for lunch this day. I have been here once before by myself. On that trip, I selected to walk the forest trails from the train station up to the Kloster. It was a good decision once, but I wouldn't do it again, unless you want that day of exercise in the fresh air. But, exercise only makes you more thirsty, and you are probably thirsty already.

The train ride is quick, clean, and inexpensive. The bus ride is slow, clean, and infrequent. A taxi is also available, but expensive. The little village of Herrshing is cute and worth a walk around, if you are waiting for the bus. The Lake Ammersee is picturesque and a short walk from the train station.

Andechs is known for its fabulous beers and tasty Bavarian food specialties. When you walk into the pub or the restaurant you will be impressed with the atmosphere and the views. The smell of food, and the clanging sound of glass mugs is in the air. You can sit either inside or outside.

Nina and I are ready for lunch, but a taste of that beer is the priority now.

The prices for both the food and the beer at the kloster are inexpensive. Mostly, it is help yourself. Go to a ticket window, purchase a ticket for the size beer you want, and move a couple steps to where the beer is being poured. Two men in blue aprons are "barreling" today. The helles, light gold beer, and the dunkels, dark brown beer, are pouring from wooden kegs! Fresh beer served from a wooden keg. It just doesn't get any better. We both skip the helles, and go for the dunkel. One half-liter for only 3 Euros.

The dunkel, at 4.8% alcohol, had a warm gold brown color, full foamy tan head, and had a velvety texture in the mouth. Delicious. Andechs calls their dunkel beer "double bock light". A little bit of sarcasm there. They also brew a doppelbock dunkel at 7%, but I have only seen it served in bottles. I have heard a rumor, that the doppelbock is no longer served from the keg here because of over consumption problems. It didn't matter to us the dunkel was perfect.

We grabbed a table outside to sit. There was a chill in the air on this sunny winter day. There was a small amount of snow piled in the corners of the deck. We kept our jackets on and the dark beers warmed us up. The views of the rolling hills on one side of us, and the steeple of the church on the other side of us are spectacular. The beers went down quickly.

It's time for food. You can help yourself by walking up to a cafeteria like area and getting a good look at what is available to eat. It's easy to see there are hearty portions of Bavarian specialties. A glance up at the menu board and you quickly realize the prices are inexpensive. They have food selections perfect for matching with beer. Kloster made cheeses, breads, salami, and sausages, along with crisp grilled pork roast, and grilled knuckle of pork. The side dishes for the main courses are meals in themselves and tasty. This is a beer friendly place.

When we were finished eating, and about to order our next round of beers, I noticed that Nina was intently watching the guys pour the beers from the wooden keg. She wondered how they got back behind the counter and she began looking for a door. I didn't think too much about looking for that door, and I got on line to buy another beer ticket. As I stepped away from the cashier, and over to the barrels, I am shocked to see Nina behind the counter! She is using sign language to ask the draftsmen if she can pour her own beer. They both have big smiles on their faces and obviously agree to this plot. Of course, this is when I arrive at the counter to get my beer. I grab my camera and get a great shot of Nina pouring the beer. Nina then hands me the beer, and without hesitation asks for the beer ticket. The two guys working figured out that we were together and got a great laugh out of it all. She stayed and poured a few more before returning to the other side.

We found a spot near the barrels at a stand up table. No one was eating in this area, just enjoying the beer. The Kloster Andechs beer slogan is "Pleasure for the body and soul". Yes it is. In this area, we were able to have a few conversations with others and meet some interesting people. However, the clock is ticking and we have a dinner reservation in the evening at Weisses Brauhaus back in Munich.

We finish our last beer and walk a few minutes to the bus stop. When we checked the posted bus schedule, we realized we broke a major rule of traveling; always know your return time for the bus or the train before your drinking session begins! The bus had just departed and the next bus was not for another hour. Okay, no problem, back up the hill into the braustuberl for another dunkel. Have you ever noticed that time seems to go by so fast when you're enjoying a great beer with great company? Surprisingly, the hour speeds by, and we run down to the bus stop. Exactly an hour has passed again, and we miss the bus again. I'm not going into that Kloster again! Let's call a taxi.

Coincidentally, there was a taxi parked nearby. We approach the taxi and try to get a ride to the train station. The driver tells us that she is waiting for someone that called for a lift. So we decide to wait for the next bus, at the bus stop. Several minutes pass and the taxi driver waves us over. Her ride has not appeared (of course not, they are drinking some dunkels) and she is willing to take us now. We jump in and arrive at the train station quickly.

The schedule tells us we have about a fifteen-minute wait for the train, so we just wander around the station. It seems there is a mini-biergarten set up along the tracks in an area of landscaping. There is even a stammtisch table made on top of an old tree stump, on which there is a plaque crediting the builders and welcoming all travelers to share it. I just can't believe that there has to be a biergarten everywhere, and every biergarten has to have a stammtisch. What dedication the Bavarians have to their beer drinking.

Soon the S-Bahn arrives and we know that we have 30 minutes to nap on the train before arriving back in Munich. Remember, we are having dinner at Weisses Brauhaus. It's a reserved dinner with the brewer of the famous Schneider Bros. weisse beers, scheduled through my sales representative at Stuff Yer Face.

It's time to rally!

WEISSES BRAUHAUS

Luckily for us, our hotel is just two blocks from the Hauptbahnhof, the main train station, in Munich. We run back to our room for a very fast freshening up, and need to walk fast to make the reservation on time.

Weisses is located on Tal Strasse. To get there we need to walk through the Marienplatz, and towards the Isartor Gate on the East side of the Platz. The building, which houses Weisses Brauhaus, was a brewery as early as 1540. Georg Schneider bought the location in 1872 to brew his weisse beers. It is located just around the corner from the famous Hofbrauhaus. The Schneider Weisse beers are readily available in the USA including the Original and the dark, or stark, Aventinus.

We are going to arrive just on time for our reservation, however, a little exhausted from our afternoon at Kloster Andechs. As I mentioned, our reservation was made through my beer salesperson at my restaurant, Stuff Yer Face. We have been selling Schneider products for several years. We are not sure whom, if anyone, we are meeting at the restaurant. As we are met at the door, it is explained to us that we are meeting Hans Peter Drexler, the Brewmaster of Schneider. This is a pleasant surprise to us. I guess he will just stop by the table to say hello and welcome us.

I have been to the Brauhaus several times on previous trips to Munich. It is a very nice place, smaller than the other brauhauses belonging to the larger Munich brewers, but it comes with a lot of atmosphere. During the day the outside area is usually filled with beer drinkers.

The restaurant's food is highly regarded within the city. Many tourists will eat a good dinner here, and then move on to the ruckus festivities of the Hofbrauhaus. The menu is very extensive and we know the beers are simply top notch. Nina and I are here just to enjoy a hearty Bavarian meal and call it quits for the evening.

We are escorted through the first floor pub area and up a flight of stairs and enter a very fashionable dining room. The room is very Bavarian looking with the amber lighting, wood wainscoting, wooden furniture, and historical photos on the walls and collectable krugs in cabinets, white tablecloths and the Bavarian blue and white napkins on the tables.

Just after getting the menu Mr. Hans Drexler arrives and welcomes us. Luckily, he speaks English very well. To our surprise, he sits at the table and we learn that he is joining us for dinner. I'm happy about that. He soon helps us with the menu and describes some of the entrees. It was a good thing that he did, because Nina and I were about to order a plate that was described as a sampling. We weren't sure what we would be sampling until Hans explained it was the organs of the pig. Okay, we're adventurous, but not for that, tonight. I ask him his favorite dish, or the specialty of the house and he recommends the roasted goose. It will be my first goose, and I'm looking forward to it.

Our first beer selection was the Schneider Original. They were delivered in the tall weisse glass with a large white head on top. The Original is 5.4% alcohol, has an amber mahogany color, with aromas of clove, nutmeg, and apples. It is crisp, clean, very refreshing, and noticeably tastier than the beer from the bottle at home. He is quite proud of this beer, which was the first brewed by Georg Schneider in 1872.

While we are waiting for our food to arrive at the table, we go on a tour of the building. The first stop is down to the basement to see the keg cooler. The cooler was spotless, with almost 100 kegs stacked from the floor to the ceiling. Hans mentioned that rotation of the kegs was very important, and strictly followed here. Then we went up a flight of stairs, through the kitchen area, and out to the bar area where the beers are poured.

Of course I got my chance to pull a weisse beer for some unlucky customer in the pub. The first attempt resulted in a glass full of foam. I forgot how lively a weisse beer is and I didn't use the proper technique. The second pour was nearly perfect, and I was allowed to drink it. Here I was, pouring my own Schneider Weisse Original in Munich, Germany. That beer tasted so good.

Our dinners arrived, and the portions were huge. The food was delicious, as is usual anywhere in Munich. The goose was excellent, and served with a beer sauce.

Our next round of beer was first the Aventinus, dark wheat, 8.2% alcohol from the cask. I believe that this version of the Aventinus is that which is available in the USA, but mostly by the bottle. It has a dark ruby color, a chocolate aroma, and has hints of banana, raisins, and caramel in the taste. It is just slightly bitter. It's fabulous to follow with after the Original. The second beer at the table was the Aventinus Eisbock from a bottle with a purple label on it. This is a slightly stronger version of the regular Aventinus at 12% alcohol. The tastes were similar, but with a hint of more spices and the taste of the alcohol.

Nina and I totally enjoyed the food and the beer and were ready to throw in the napkin when some schnaps arrived at the table. It seems that Schneider is now making a schnaps, Aventinus Edelbrand, that is 42% alcohol. It is served in a miniature Aventinus shaped glass. I was a little apprehensive to drink it, given the kind of day that we have had today, but I couldn't resist, and I didn't want to appear rude. The Edelbrand was clear and had a fruity flavor to it. It seems Hans is especially proud of the Edelbrand and soon wants another. One more for us too, and that's it! I was very surprised that Nina drank those two glasses of schnaps. She whispered in my ear for me not to be surprised, because she didn't actually drink them. The glasses were empty, so where did they go? She never told me.

It was a terrific visit to Weisses Brauhaus. It must be on your list of stops if you visit Munich. If you are walking down Tal Strasse you'll first recognize the giant Schneider Original Weisse beer bottle standing outside. Give it a hug before you walk in, it makes for a great photo.

COLOGNE and DUSSELDORF, GERMANY

Most people recognize Cologne's skyline on the Rhine River, where the massive 750-year-old Cathedral dominates. But, lying in the shadows of the Dom is the culture of Brauhaus life and beer tradition.

Visiting Cologne is like going to your friend's house that has decided to throw a themed party. Beer is the basis of the party, only one style of beer, served a certain way, in a certain glass, along with a certain style of food, while speaking a special dialect developed just for the party. If you do not like any features of the theme, you can't go else where because the whole town does the same thing up and down its streets. There is no variation on the theme, just different faces and smiles to meet. But, Cologne throws such a good party you will want to stay. Staying is like living at the perfect party. While at the party you can have a job, go food shopping, get your car fixed, or go to the dentist...all the regular things you do in life, except it's all during the party.

Cologne, or Koln, is located on the banks of the Rhine River. Once a "colony" of the Roman Empire it was founded around AD 50. The majority of the people are Catholics as opposed to Protestants being the majority in the rest of Germany. The people of Koln speak their own dialect of Deutsch called Kolsch and brew a style of beer also called Kolsch. They say Kolsch is the only language you can drink. As they say in Kolsch "Drink doch ene met" or "drink one with me!" The Kolners pride themselves on being warm and friendly. Historically they were the first to adopt the Catholic religion and the last to recognize the Nazi Party before World War II. Occasionally the Rhine River overflows its banks and floods the city. The one million inhabitants take it in stride without any anger or regrets and say, "It is what it is."

Cologne *is what it is*. You won't find too much variety here when it comes to beer. They have been brewing for 1000 years. Stop in a pub and you are expected to drink the famous Kolsch beer. A top fermented, delicate, tangy, pale gold color, lively beer that must by law be brewed within the city limits to be called Kolsch. Koln is a city of 156 square miles and 24 breweries, that is one brewery for every 40,000 people. Each brewery has its own slightly different variation on the taste of the Kolsch beer. Germany has some great beers within some great beer style categories, but, just as they did with their Deutsch dialect the Kolsch developed their own beer style.

At first taste, you might think you would get bored with the beer, but it seems to grow on you. It's subtle flavors are very appealing, satisfying, and almost medicinal. The slight bitterness of the hops is balanced pleasantly with the sweetness of the malt. It has a pretty yellow gold color and a very friendly white foam top. It seems to smile at you just like the people of the town.

Each pour of Kolsch is served in a unique .2 liter glass, called a stange. A waiter, called a Kobes, carrying a Kranz, delivers it to you. The whole process is so unique. These Kolners have really planned the theme of their party.

The stang is a specially shaped glass, that is tall and narrow, about five inches tall and two inches in diameter. It's holds five ounces in volume. You can't get a pint, so don't even ask. The Kobesse are very friendly gents, usually wearing about the same uniform no matter where you stop, a blue shirt and a dark apron around their waist. While your drinking your first Kolsch you know that you will have another. So how do the Kobesse keep up with service of those little beers?

The pub is filled with customers, and everyone is drinking Kolsch. No martinis, no wine, not even a pint of Guinness to be seen. See, this is the themed party I was talking about. Your host, the Kolsch people, have you doing things their way.

So it is time to order another Kolsch. That first little one goes down quickly. Before you start looking around for the Kobes, he is at your side. He knows that your glass is just a sip away from being empty. He carries with him, his secret weapon, the Kranz. Again, a unique design twist on the normal, everyday serving tray. The Kranz is a two level tray which carefully nestles about a dozen stangs. It has a tall center handle, which enables the Kobes to quickly dance around the pub without spilling a precious drop of the Kolsch beer.

Walk the streets of the old town area and this drinking scenario is carried out exactly the same in every pub. Kolsch beer has a 90% market share here. If you don't like the theme of this party, you'll have to leave town, because "it is what it is" here. However, you will like it, in fact, I think you will love it!

The host of this party is fun, friendly and interesting. The next thing the Kolsch people impress you with is their food. The food of the pub is listed on the "foderkaat" or menu. Of course, the food too is just slightly different than the rest of Germany's.

Nina and I visited Koln in the Spring of 2006. I had stopped in once before by myself a few years earlier and was familiar with the beer and the Kobes. I had not really met the people though until my visit with Nina. We arrive after the night time trans-atlantic flight at 8am. It's tough to start the day after a sleepless night, but you must do it. Stay awake and take only a short nap. It is better to quickly get adjusted to the time difference and get on the local time schedule. Nina and I did a quick walking tour of the city just to see the Rhine River, the giant Dom and just get a general feel for the city. The Cathedral took over 750 years to build and always seems to be under renovation. Within it's walls are the Relics of the Three Wise Men. It's basic structure survived the massive bombings of the Allied forces during World War II because of a distinct decision by the pilots to save the Cathedral.

While walking the streets of Old Town, or Altstadt, you will notice the cozy feel of the winding streets. One of our first stops was a small bookstore. I picked up a 64-page brochure entitled "The Cologne Brauhaus Trail" by Franz Mathar. The book describes a brewery tour for the tourist to follow. This is the perfect world. The tour takes you past the museums, churches, and of course the pubs. It mentions the names of the brewers Sunner, Paffgen, Goffel, Sion, Dom, Sohn, and Peter's.

Nina picked up a postcard entitled "Das Kolsche Grundgesetz" which listed ten favorite sayings of the Kolsch people that describes the character of the townspeople. A light bulb goes off in our heads, and we have an idea. We are going on the described pub crawl, and we will get this post card translated into English so we can better understand the Kolsch people. We think that with a little help from bartenders, the Kobes, and new friends we meet along the way, we will get these sayings translated for us to English.

Our first stop is Peter's Brauhaus just in time for an early lunch, or breakfast as it may be. Peter's is one of the larger brauhauses in town, and is very woodsy along with stained glass ceilings in some rooms. In the center of the main room is what is called the Thekenschaaf or confessional. It looks like something from a church, but is where the owner sits to keep an eye on business and do some paperwork at the same time. The smaller room on the side has a stained glass ceiling and wood wainscoting. This is a room I could sit and drink Kolsch all day long in.

The Kobes approaches the table in his traditional uniform and gives us a wide smile. We're the only customers at the moment. Of course, two Kolsch please. The first sip of the beer was just great after that long long flight across the ocean. Kolsch is a great first beer of the day and it only cost 1,20 Euro. We review the menu, or foodorkaat, and notice that menu items are written in both the Kolsch dialect and the Deutsch language. Our first order is sauerkraut soup with pork sausage, "Rheinische sauerkrautsuppe mit mettwurst", and "wirsing", savoy cabbage browned and almost creamy like. Both were delicious. We were happy to make this stop.

We look around the rooms and estimate that it must seat several hundred. There is lots of history on the walls with black and white photos. I noticed a poster on the wall for a Beethoven concert in 1914. Directly seated below the poster was a local student with his WIFI in action. Nothing like enjoying today's technology in a traditional setting. A few more Kolsch beers and some sausage and we start up a conversation with the Kobes. He gives us our first translation on the post card. The first saying is "Et es wie et es" which translates to "it is what it is". A fine Jimmy Buffet type attitude here in Cologne. The Kobes got a laugh from the post card and so did we. We already feel at home here.

Nina and I visit a couple of other pubs while dodging the raindrops. Each pub serves a different Kolsch, same size glass, and same friendly smile. I like this town. In the middle of the afternoon, we are near the Dom and stop in at the Dom Hotel, which has, a modern bar named Peter Ustinov's. Businessmen and women dressed in their business attire drinking their Kolsch. We have a friendly bartender from Poland. Surprisingly, he offers his help in some translations on the post card. He has been in town for only a year, but has learned to love it and the people. He struggles with a few of the phrases because they really aren't properly translated as most slang is not. But he takes the card around to other customers and his boss and gets us the second and third of the sayings. "It comes when it comes" and "nothing stays the way it is". Just a few simple sayings that the Kolsch people pride themselves on for a style of life, and it is evident to us after just one morning and afternoon.

In the evening, we make our way to Brauhaus Sion, another of the large, well-established pubs that brew and sell the Kolsch beer. The food is supposed to be good here. The Sion beer is one of the better ones. There are just slight differences in all of them, and you'll find the one you prefer. The menu looks good to me because it has a "Unsere Wurstecke", or sausage corner. I just think that you can't beat the German sausage makers as the sausage matches perfectly with their beer. It seems that locally throughout Germany the sausage seasoning change slightly to match the locally brewed beer style.

Also on the menu is a local item, "Halven Hahn", which literally translates to half a chicken, but is a rye bread roll with butter and a piece of cheese. A really good appetizer for eating while drinking a beer. Simple, delicious, and satisfying. We wander around the Old Town a little longer, but then it is time for sleep. Maybe it will stop raining tomorrow.

The next morning brings us a clear blue sky so we walk across a bridge to the other side of the River. From the East side of the Rhine you get a fantastic view of the Old Town and the Dom. There is a promenade along both sides of the Rhine for easy touring. We stop for a tour of the Lindts Chocolate factory. It is very informative, and smells good, but they don't serve any beer.

So we're off for lunch. Picking a spot for lunch is easy. It can be anywhere. The food is good, the service is good, and the beer is good. We stop in at Brauhaus Paffgen. Nina and I share a rosti, which is a large potato pancake-like item with items added such as bacon and smoked salmon. Perfect with the Kolsch! The waiter is from Greece and he too helps further with our postcard translations.

We visited the world famous Eau de Cologne original offices and factory in the Old Town area. Good tour, but no beer here either. It begins to rain again, so just a few doors away is a place called Ech Kolsch. Not a typical woodsy pub, but a newer looking place, with a woman behind the bar. Having a bar is not typical for the region. While traveling, you get use to sitting at the large tables and waiting for service. To sit at a bar is unusual.

The woman behind the bar is very friendly to us from the start. She is serving Sion Kolsch. We find that her name is Angelica and that she, along with her husband, are the owners. She explains to us that Sion is the best beer to drink here and that the name of her establishment means "real". Angelica and her husband try to uphold the traditions for food of the area. She seems very knowledgeable and explains the story of why the "halven hahn" is really not an order of a half chicken. As the legend goes, a Princess or Queen offered all her subjects dinner, but soon realized she didn't have enough for them all, so she had to improvise, and served them only bread and cheese.

We offer to purchase her a beer and she agrees, so we are hitting it off. She returns the favor of the gratuitous beer with an offer for the local blood sausage. Now I am a lover of sausage, and so is Nina, but I have not tried the blood sausage. But we gladly accept the offer, expecting a small slice to share. Angelica returns from the kitchen with a plate of sliced blood sausage. Enough for a meal. We dive into the plate enthusiastically and give it a taste. Not as bad as I expected, but not something I would order again. We were polite and struggled to finish the serving. We got FREE blood sausage! Nina said it had to be *free* or she wouldn't have eaten it.

I started a conversation with a gentleman at the bar and learned a new word for my beer vocabulary. He was describing to me that tomorrow was a local religious holiday and that many pubs would be closed. There were however, several outdoor festivals to go to at some of the smaller churches. He told me that he would be "barreling" tomorrow. That is, he was working the tap and serving the beers. I like that word.

Nina was talking it up with Angelica and working on the translations of the post card. Angelica was really good at the translations and could have finished it up for us, but that would have taken all the fun out of it. She knew her history well and was very proud to be Kolsch. She was also a great hostess.

Just before leaving and saying goodbye, our new friends reminded us that tomorrow was a holiday and recommended a pub that would still be open. It sounded as if it was going to be something like a Father's Day celebration. We thanked them for the tip and ventured out into the Altstadt.

It wasn't more than a few yards when we came upon a very busy place with people practically busting out of the open windows. The rain had stopped, the sun was coming out and it was late Friday afternoon. Happy Hour! The pub's name was Brauhaus Sunner. We were met at the door by a sea of people. All of the seats at the tables were taken so we ventured into the stube area. A very tiny lean to bar area with about 4 tables near the windows.

We located two seats along side two elderly gents enjoying their Kolsch. I don't remember how the conversation started, but it was within seconds. Prost! Not too much English was spoken but they gave a round of free beer to us. They didn't stay very long. Just before leaving we exchanged toasts with "Prost" and "Cheers" and "Good luck". Three co-workers standing nearby overheard us and began to add their own words for cheers. The Greek, "Yamas", the Hungarian, "Eggeh shegeh dreh", the Turkish, "Sher ee feh" and South African, "Optikahanyas". Our new friends Kostas, Liliana, and Selmouch were well traveled and worked together at the airport. We shared quite a few rounds of Kolsch.

As the sun was setting Nina and I were invited out for dinner with them. We accepted the invite. They recommended the Brauhaus Sion because the food was very good. Nina and I were proud to announce that we had found this place the night before. As usual the food was excellent. We all exchanged emails and said an early good night.

The next day was the Father's Day holiday and a little drizzly. Around the Altstadt were many men, sons, fathers, and grandfathers walking the streets and along the river. Soon the pubs would fill up I'm sure. Nina and I found Haxenhaus zum Rheingarten near the River that was open and active at lunchtime. It's a nice cozy place, the kind of place that really works for us on a rainy day. We have grown fond of the local soups on the menu, usually goulash, onion, or sauerkraut. Each is a meal in itself and goes perfectly with the beer. The chatter in the place was loud and lively.

On the way to the toilette near the stairs I noticed a poster on the wall. It was a photo of the old town area with the houses and buildings flooded from the river. The water level was almost ten feet deep it seemed. The words at the top of the poster read "Ett kutt, wie et kutt". They looked familiar to me. Of course, the postcard. I remember the translation as "It comes when it comes!" The Rhine River had come! So, it was worth a laugh. I would have loved to have purchased a copy of that poster. I guess I had learned my lessons well here in Cologne.

It's easy to get to Cologne. It has a major airport with direct flights from Newark, New Jersey via Continental Airlines. Train connections to Brussels are only 2½ hours, Munich is about 3½ hours, Frankfurt about 1½ hours, and Dusseldorf is less than 30 minutes.

Dusseldorf is another great beer city. It is located only 25 miles to the North of Cologne situated where the River Dussel reaches the Rhine River. There have been farming and fishing settlements there since the 7th and 8th Centuries. Dusseldorf was granted city status in 1288. There seems to be a rivalry with nearby Cologne, but nothing really in history to account for this or to label it hostile. There is a great rivalry in the city futbol teams. Both Napoleon and the Allies of World War II have destroyed Dusseldorf. More recently, it has developed into a fashion and finance powerhouse.

The most touristy or trendy street is Konigs Alle, or Kings Avenue, better known as The Ko. Most of the major shops in fashion are located here. In stark contrast are the streets of Alstadt, remnants of the old town where there are over 260 inns and restaurants. The tourism board touts the area as "the longest bar in the world". It could be, there are plenty of places to drink the famous Dusseldorf Alt beer. We'll be looking for the house brews of Uerige, Fuchschen, Schumacher, and Schlussel.

For years I have thought that Alt beer meant old style of pre-refrigeration days recipes. I have since found out that the Alt might be from the Latin "Altos" for "high", indicating the rising yeast during fermentation. The beer is a top fermenting ale with an initial hint of malt and followed with the bitterness of the hops. It is aromatic, smooth, and light brown in color, about 4.5% alcohol content. Like in

Cologne, it is a special type of beer brewed only around the city.

Nina and I reached Dusseldorf on a bright sunny Sunday morning. We had just spent the previous three nights in little towns on the Rhine River. The Rhine doesn't offer much variety in the beer selections, to our surprise, but it is a good area for German wines and beautiful scenery. The main train station in Dusseldorf is not quite as centrally located as other major cities, but easy and quick enough to reach your hotel by foot. The Altstadt area is about a 30 minute walk from the Hauptbanhoff, with plenty of hotels between the two. We check into our hotel which is directly across the street from a brauhaus and know that that will be noisy at night.

We immediately head down to the Old Town area to visit the "longest bar". It's easy to find. The crowds get larger and the streets get smaller. It seems particularly busy today. The tiny streets are almost impassible and there are bands playing live music in the streets. We notice a banner flying across one of the streets. It seems that we have wandered into a Jazz Festival! How lucky for us, it's a beautiful day.

All the pubs have their outside areas open with tables and chairs. I hate to mention that other city's name, but it reminds me of Cologne here. The Kobesse are dancing around the crowd with their Kranz held high above their heads. The trays are carrying those same small .2 liter glasses, but they are filled with a pretty brown beer. We walk by the Schlussel Brauhaus and notice two outdoor lean to's available, but decide to go inside because we need something to eat. Again, Nina and I feel most comfortable in the stube area. The stube area is where most people are standing at barrel top tables and usually drinking, but some are eating.

It is evident from the start that our Kobes is very efficient and very friendly. We quickly get our first two alts. The alts are different from the Kolsch, but very delicious and refreshing. The place is busy. The Kobes is working fast. A table of about six locals has many empties on their table. We notice that when they order a round, they add one in for the Kobe. He happily accepts the offer and downs the beer with his back to the front door and windows. He's having fun. Nina and I order a Wurstsalat. It's a cold plate with lettuce leafs, tomato, julienne sliced cooked salami tossed with a light oil and vinegar mixture along with diced pickles and parsley. Very tasty and it comes with warm roasted potatoes.

For our next round of beers we order three Alt beers, including one beer for our Kobes. He loves it, and downs it in a second. Our neighbors at the next table laugh and prost us. We contently watch trays filled with dozens of little brown filled glasses go by us. The streets are jammed. We have a good spot, but we must move on.

Dusseldorf has a promenade along the East side of the Rhine River. It is the perfect place to walk, people watch, and enjoy the sunset across the river. We have that sight in our eyes, Jazz in our ears, and Alt in our stomachs. At the North end of the promenade is a large tent set up with the main music attraction. There are many food kiosks set up selling the typical items like pretzels and bratwurst. We try to sneak into the show in the tent, but Nina gets held up by security behind me. We almost made it. I guess we're off to the next pub.

We have heard so much about Zum Uerige. Their beer is imported to the USA and is readily available at good beer shops. They also have guest rooms above the brauhaus! We make our way there, but it is very tight in the streets because they have a Jazz band playing right outside their establishment. They are playing New Orleans stuff,

Dixieland style, and old American classics. It reminds me that the USA is king of music and the Germans are the kings of brewing. We enter the brauhaus and grab some great leaning space near the fresh air of the door and directly in front of where the Zappes are working. Those are the guys who tap the beer and fill the glasses.

It's easy to get a beer no matter how busy. The Kobesse do a great job. I can't help thinking, how difficult it would be to get a beer if this was the situation somewhere in the States. I never understood the ritual at home of standing three or four deep in front of the bar trying to get the one bartender's attention for my drink. It takes so long sometimes I just want to leave.

The Uerige beer is delicious, a bit more malty than the other Alts that we have sampled. As I am watching the Zappe do his thing, I notice that the keg he is working from is wooden and sitting at eye level to him. Suddenly three other guys dressed in their blue uniforms arrive carrying another wooden keg. One Kobes has a wooden mallet in his hand and a brass spigot. He quickly places the spigot over the bunghole and whacks it with the mallet. Then the three of them lift it up into position ready for dispensing. I was happy to get three quick photos of the action. When I dropped the camera from my eye, I noticed Nina was standing right there in the middle of all the action. She was returning from the toilette, and always ends up in the right place at the right time. I review the photos, and there she is with a big smile on her face as she watches the tapping.

We wander around the Alstadt the remainder of the afternoon café to café. We find seats on a docked boat in the river and enjoy one last beer for the evening. The breeze was getting cool, but it was a near perfect day. Maybe we'll get a gelato for the walk back to the hotel.

We hit the streets early the next morning, Monday. We are a little surprised that the streets are so quiet. There is no vehicular traffic and no pedestrian traffic. We make our way to the train station to check out tomorrow's trains to the airport for connecting to our flight home. Quiet everywhere. I see a small tourist information center and decide to walk in. I purchase a guide to the beer and Alstadt area. Perfect, except it is only in Deutsch. We ask the attendant why the town is so quiet, and she informs us that today is a local religious holiday. *(Another one!)* She tells us that everyone is off work, and all the shops will be closed. We are very surprised and I quickly ask if the pubs will be open. She happily says yes, the pubs will be open.

It's a little disappointing to Nina and I that the stores will be closed today. It is our last day in Europe this trip and we had planned some shopping for gifts. The World Cup soccer tournament was being played at several venues in Germany. We wanted to purchase some team shirts, but we found that difficult to do today.

We went back to Schlussel Brauhaus for lunch because the beer was good, the people were friendly, and it was open. We ordered a Berliner Bratwurst plate with "spitzkohl", white cabbage cooked down nice and caramelized. It arrived with those famous German pan fried potatos. I guess Nina and I are easily satisfied, because a meal like that really makes our day.

We took in some sights of Dusseldorf. It's famous street the Ko is fun to walk. All the big fashion names have shops there. No beer pubs here, but an espresso or glass of champagne is easy to come by. A small river separates the two sides of the Ko with arched stoned bridges crossing at each intersection.

Later in the evening, we find ourselves in a pub in the Old Town. They have a good beer selection and good music. That's a little different from normal around here. The Zappe was working his wooden keg from the center of the room with a cooler behind him. We could see the kegs stacked up through the plastic thermal doors. When it was time to fetch another keg here, the Zappe went into the cooler and strapped a leather belt around the keg. The leather belt extends up and hooks onto a metal hook, which is attached to a rail slightly above head height. They can then walk and guide the keg hanging from the rail to the location where the Zappe is working. It is really a sight to see. It somehow brings you back in time, and, you realize that tradition is respected here in Dusseldorf.

    I had a sense that Dusseldorf was fighting tradition slightly more than Cologne. Dusseldorf has developed into a fashion, banking, and telecom world headquarters. Maybe the tourist here seemed more international than Cologne's tourist. Why cities feel that they have to make a tourist feel like they are in their own homeland perplexes me. When I travel and leave the US I want to experience the local traditions. The last thing I want to see from the US is a McDonald's or a Budweiser. A guest from Mexico doesn't want a Mexican restaurant. I'm sure an Asian doesn't want Sushi. Give us a Dusseldorf or Cologne Brauhaus the old fashion way.

    It seems Cologne is a little more content with what they have, and I don't think it will be changing anytime soon. Sure, the smaller Brauhaus might close up over time but I don't think any of their traditions are going anywhere. The Dom in Cologne has been under construction for 750 years. The people of Cologne think that if it was ever actually finished, the world would come to an end. So, they keep building.

BRUSSELS, ANTWERP, and GHENT, BELGIUM

People use many phrases to describe the beers of Belgium. For beer lovers, Belgium is "heaven on earth" or "a beer drinkers paradise". There is even a website named beerparadise that is worth a visit.

Why? Because, this country offers a wide and rich variety of styles of beer. From the lambics, a wild, spontaneously fermenting brew, to the fruit infused beers, to the refreshing white, or wheat ales, to the taste bursting spiced ales, and the blessed Trappist ales that the monks give us. There are some good lagers or pilsners, better than the mass-produced American beers, but not comparable to the lagers of Germany or Czech Republic.

There are probably as many glass shapes in Belgium to match the beers available. Each beer must be drunk from the proper glass shape to enhance the tasting of the flavors of the beer. This practice is strictly followed, no matter where you are drinking.

The Belgians, both young and old, love their beer. In the international beer consumption competition they usually rank in the middle of the top ten countries at about 93 liters per person, per year consumed. Belgium has a total population of 10.4 million and has about 115 breweries within it's borders.

What wine is to France, beer is to Belgium. The Belgians drink quality beer.

One important reason for visiting Belgium is to be able to find, purchase, and taste the Trappist Beers. The Trappist beers are not exactly a style of beer, but more a distinct grouping of beers. In the USA these beers are difficult to locate and purchase, and some are never available. The Belgian beers are hardly ever on a restaurant menu, sometimes they can be found in a good beer bar, and occasionally they can be found in a liquor store. Yet, these beers are known the world over for their great taste and high quality due to the monks following strict traditions of brewing. If you find one in the USA, it will be expensive.

The name Trappist originates over 900 years ago from the monks of the Cistercian order of Normandy, France. There are three conditions that must be met to use the name Trappist on a bottle of beer; First, the beer must be brewed within a Trappist Abbey, second, the beer must be brewed under the supervision and responsibility of the monks, and third, the majority of the revenue produced must be dedicated to charitable work.

Seven beers can legally use the name Trappist. They include six monasteries in Belgium; Achel, Chimay, Orval, Rochefort, Westmalle, Westvleteren, and one located in the Netherlands, La Trappe. Only these seven can place the brown hexagonal logo of "Authentic Trappist Product" on their bottles. Once you find one of these beers, you have something delicious and special in your hands.

The different styles that these seven brew can vary. They can be dark or gold in color, spicy or malty in flavor, and usually they are high in alcohol content. Typically, the brew is bottle conditioned which means a second dose of yeast and sugar are added in the bottle before capping. A second fermentation then takes place within the bottle, and these beers will most likely taste better with age. The naming of the beers varies also. Chimay has a red, blue, and white version. Westmalle has a dubbel and a triple. Rochefort has a #6, #8 and #10. La Trappe sells under the label Koningshoeven in the USA, and they produce several styles including a quadruple. Rest assured, that while drinking these beers, your taste buds will be thanking you.

Other beers labeled "abbey" beers are probably very tasty also, but specifically are not Trappist beers. They may be recipes from an abbey, or from a monastery not associated with the Trappists.

Lambic is another style of beer found in Belgium. Lambic beers are also wheat beers, which use wild yeasts for fermentation. Some of these yeasts are found in the air and the wood of the buildings of where they are brewed. Typically, these beers originate only in the area around Brussels. The beers have a winey taste and are somewhat still. Another style, gueuze, is a blend of both young and old lambics. They are naturally carbonated, and to me, take on a sour taste. I have not learned to appreciate the flavors of gueuze, but if you find a pub that specializes in it don't hesitate to give it a try.

On your travels, you may also come across a fruit infused lambic beer. Tastes of raspberries, framboise, or cherries, kriek, are prominent in these beers that are highly carbonated and champagne like.

The Belgian lager Stella Artois, and the wit, or wheat, Hoegaarden are now very popular on the East Coast of the USA. These are easy drinking flavorful brews for everyday drinking.

So, a Travels for Beer to Belgium is necessary after sampling any of these beers in the USA. You will be shocked and impressed with the flavor profiles of these beers after tasting them in their homeland. Just remember, you will find yourself sipping on a beer that may be seven, nine, or eleven percent alcohol. Proceed with caution!

BRUSSELS
Brussels, which is more than a 1000 years old, is now a city of international flair. It is the European Capital and home of

the EU, the European Union. Two languages are spoken here, Dutch and French. Street signs are posted in both languages. Of course Belgium is known for their vast array of high end beers and their culinary skills. I heard it said somewhere in my travels that the Belgians can cook as well as the French, and they can eat with an appetite of a German.

If you are in Brussels for the first time, make your way to the main city plaza named Grand Place. Grand Place is just a five-minute walk from Gare Midi, the closest train station in the center of the city.

"One of the most beautiful town squares in Europe, if not in the world", is a phrase often heard when visitors in Brussels try to describe the beauty of the central market square. French-speakers refer to it as "Grand Place", whereas in Dutch it is called "de grote Markt".

Seven streets enter the Grand Place. The two larger buildings on the plaza are the Town Hall first built in 1402 and the Kings House, which now houses the City Museum. Surrounding these two buildings are ornate buildings of the different trade guilds. One of the guild buildings is home to the Brewery Museum, which is worth a visit and open everyday. Sorry, no free samples are served here!

Stand in the middle of the square and look around. Take in the architecture and notice the details. There is a mix of Gothic and Art Nouveau styles. If it is early in the morning vendors may be setting up their vegetables or flowers for market, or if it is in the evening, you may experience a fantastic sunset. Grand Place would be your best bet for your first experience of Belgian cuisine. Choose any café, they are all good. A menu is usually posted outside so you can judge the items and the prices. Some of the cafes have an outside area to sit in, or if you prefer, some have a fireplace inside to sit near. It's your choice. Don't get ripped off on the price of the moules. The mussels are served everywhere, and are tasty everywhere, but the price varies.

Nina and I have enjoyed a rainy day lunch at La Brouette on the second floor. La Brouette, meaning the Wheelbarrow is the house of the guild of the graissiers. The best I can figure is that this is the guild of candle makers. There is an open fire pit, old wooden window frames, a wood floor worn to a fine patina, and well-dressed waiters. It is a great place to sit with a quietly drawn pils or a special Belgian beer.

We both shared a delicious salad Nicoise and a Ciney Blonde and Bruges Blanche biers. We sat by the window overlooking the Grand Place with the window open on this rainy day. It was a spectacular view watching the people quickly crossing the plaza with their colorful umbrellas open. The Ciney is not one of the spectacular Belgian beers, but it is a good-looking beer with a slightly orange gold color, soft spiciness, and an airy white head. The white beer from the city of Bruges, Brugs Blanche was classic tasting, non-filtered, 4.8% alcohol.

I wanted to visit two specific cafes while in Brussels. They are Cirio and Falstaff. Both come highly recommended from other travelers.

Cirio is a refined brasserie, located behind Grand Place's western end, on rue de la Bourse, directly across the street from the Brussels Stock Exchange (the Bourse). It is filled with well-dressed businesspeople, drinking away a hectic day. Cirio is a beautiful café with an outstanding Art Nouveau decor that was once part of a classy Europe-wide chain set up in 1903 by Italian canned-food magnate Francesco Cirio. It is particularly cozy and twinkling in the winter, and you'll get a real taste of Brussels in its turn-of-the-last-century mood.

It is like walking back into the 1930's. The walls are of glossy finished mahogany, and clear clean glass, trimmed in polished brass. The light fixtures are dust free with frosted glass shades. The lighting and colors create that warm feeling that welcomes.

A tuxedo dressed waiter will greet you with the bar towel lapped over his arm in case of any accidental spillage. The beer list that is offered is a feast for the eyes of an American wanting to taste the local beers. Mainly there are the more recognized brews, but they are at such ridiculously low prices, despite the bad exchange rate of the Euro and dollar.

Shortly after ordering a Rochefort 8 and a Bon Secours, the waiter appears quickly perfectly balancing a small wooden inlaid tray, trimmed with brass. On it are our selected beers, two glasses of special shapes emblazoned with the logo of our beers, and a small silver soufflé cup filled with enough peanuts for two to just nibble on. Napkins, of course, are also dropped off.

The beers are treated with such respect! Delivered 20 feet from the bar to you on an elaborate tray, delicately placed on the table, to be drank from the perfect vessel, and accompanied by a salty food to enhance the taste of the beer. What perfection! What a way to drink, taste and experience the world's greatest beers! Taking that first sip, rolling the beer over the tongue, and hesitating to swallow, makes you understand why the ritual and respect for the service.

My first beer here was the Bon Secours Ambree, from Brasserie Caulier the "Biere Vivante". I enjoyed this on the outside patio. It was so tasty I had to wonder why I had never heard of it, or tasted it before. The label tells me 8%, it pours with an amber gold color, has a thick white head, herbal smells on the nose, and tastes of caramel and cognac. I would love to drink this frequently.

The Rochefort 8, a Trappist ale, is 9% alcohol, dark brown in color, has a soft body, almost creamy, that is dry, and has a fruitiness to it, including hints of figs. A spectacular beer.

Falstaff, my second choice of pubs to visit, is located on Rue Henri Mausstraat, also near the Bourse, and is easily confused with Cirio after you have visited each a few times and had a few Trappist ales. The interior design here is slightly more grandiose.

In the rear is a room with large tables and is lighted with the use of stained glass in the ceiling and on the wall. The ceiling is composed of a large glass panel featuring a segmented circle using the colors of wheat, gold, cream and burgundy.

The most remarkable elements of the decorations are the two stained glass picture windows on the back wall of the main room. They depict some street scenes from the turn of the century and were built in 1906 and 1916 when the Falstaff success required renovations.

The name Falstaff came from Sir John Falstaff, diplomat and British Captain from the Royal Family. Sir Falstoff was known in London to be a big drinker, eater, and player. William Shakespaere created a character with the same name and habits in the theater piece, Henry V. Orson Wells played this character. The portrait of Falstaff is in the center between the two large picture windows in the back of the main room. The room is finished off with a large centered chandelier with teardrop crystal fixtures and mirrors and sconces on the walls.

The beer menu has enough variety, and includes some of the Trappist ales. Snacks are available, and of course you will get your little personal size serving of peanuts to go with your beer!

I shouldn't tell you where our next favorite place is, because it is more fun to find it yourself. But, the name is Au Bon Vieux Temps or "To the Good Old Times".

You will find window-shopping easy to do in Brussels. Brussels is known for its chocolates and lace shops. In an early evening of strolling and looking in the shop windows we turn a corner from a very old church, Eglise St. Nicolas, and spot a Corsendonk neon sign about 50 feet down this tiny three foot wide alley. We figure there must be a bar down there. Should we go? At a moment like this you have to trust your beer gut feeling, your sixth sense.

We don't see anyone either leaving or entering the door. We approach and give the heavy wooden door a heave. It opens to a quiet room filled with cigarette smoke. It's dark but we can see it is a small bar with about six stools in a room with eight booths and tables. An elderly woman is sitting at a large table speaking with several other people. We make our way to the bar.

The bar has all the right signage. Trappist beer signs! A bar to sit at in Europe is also fairly rare. You become quite accustomed to sitting at large tables and share the space. There is a small copper kettle behind us. The walls are lined with old dark wood. No one else is in the bar. The elderly woman from the table goes behind the bar and asks us what we would like to drink. We select a Duvel and a Westmalle from the list. They were not expensive, about $4 each.

Duvel is a fantastic golden ale with a strength of 8%. It is served up in it's own tulip shaped glass emblazoned with its logo. The glass is shaped to gather the extra frothy bright white head. It smells of hops and has a fruity spicy taste. The Westmalle dubbel, or double, is a Trappist ale. Dark brown in color, 7%, it is smooth, has a rounded mouth feel, and complex fruit flavors. The beer is bottle conditioned with a second dose of sugar and yeast added before bottling. It is one of my favorites.

We had a couple of rounds there and soaked in the atmosphere of the place. No one else arrived while we were there, and the group at the table must have been discussing something very serious because they never lifted their heads from conversation. We called it a night.

On another trip to Brussels, we had planned a day trip to find the Westmalle Monastery. It is not possible to taste the beers there, but across the street from the entrance is a café which serves the freshest of Westmalle on tap. Westmalle dubbel from the bottle is one of my top five beers of the world, and I can not imagine it flowing from a tap.

The evening before our planned day trip to Westmalle, we were walking the crowded streets of Brussels. We had already been to our favorite places and spent the afternoon at a new find, the Metropole Hotel. Where do we go next? Just as we are about to call it a night, we see a dimly lit Corsendonk neon sign at the end an alley. Nina and I both remember that we have been here before. A very small place that seemed to be run by two elderly ladies.

We enthusiastically pull open the heavy wooden door and are greeted with a cloud of cigarette smoke. We brush it aside and we knew we had stumbled upon one of our favorite beer bars, Au Bon Vieux Temps. Yes indeed, to the good old times!

This time the place was busy. We were able to get the last vacant table, and noticed a beer list that we hadn't noticed on our first visit. The menu listed Westmalle dubbel and Triple on tap! The price was just 2,50 Euro, that's about $3.25. This would be the first time for me to taste Westmalle from the tap. They were smooth and delicious, but not as well rounded as the bottle versions which are bottle conditioned. Behind us was a group of eight people ordering Duvel rounds, several rounds.

Two elderly women seem to run this place, one behind the bar, and the other running the tables. There is a great atmosphere here, and great beers. We could sit here all night. We nearly did. We need to cancel the day trip to Westmalle, because we found it on tap here in Brussels. I push my luck with my last order and ask for a bottle of Westvleteren, the most difficult Trappist beer to find. The woman leaned over and whispered into my ear. She stated that if I find any Westvleteren anywhere to be sure and tell her where. Well, at least I asked.

The Metropole is a grand hotel located at 31 Place de Brouckere. Room rates are not too bad, considering, and we agree some day to return as guests. It is 110 years old and meticulously refinished to match the ritzy, glitzy décor of that time. We came across the hotel on again, another rainy day. We wanted to go to a museum, but it was just too far in the pouring rain. We'll just sit tight here and enjoy those delicious 9% beers.

The Metropole has a large outside seating area that is covered by an awning. The tables and seats are packed rather tightly together, but it feels cozy. There are some heaters for this cooler weather.

There are brasserie type snacks on the menu and some super sweets to try. We stick with the beer. We have just arrived from Cologne this particular morning and had been drinking Kolsch beer for three days. It is quite a change from Kolsch to a Belgian ale.

Inside the pub area is just exquisite. There is something about those warm wood tones, with amber lighting, brass highlights and red fabrics that make me want to settle in.

The dark wood here is used on the walls from the floor to the ceiling and then on the ceiling also. The wood is highly figured, with lots of moldings and details. The walls are broken up with huge arched mirrors that are framed with the wood. The ceiling is ornate with moldings and carvings.

The large, almost wooden like, chandeliers throughout the room cast an amber gold glow of light. There are wooden coat racks placed against the wooden pillars that are spaced out through the room. The pillars have green ferns sprouting from the tops.

Throughout the room there are low semi-round booths of burgundy colored faux leather. The tables are wooden. The waiters, no waitresses, are scurrying around dressed in their long sleeved white shirts, black vests, and black bow ties.

In the center of the room, blocking a main aisle way, is a table displaying the fancy desserts. The menu at the tables only offers snacks, great accompaniment to the beers. The beer list is good, with a nice variety to choose from.

Rain or shine, the Metropole is a place to spend some time, inside or outside.

We definitely had had enough to drink towards the end of this day and evening in Brussels. Those 9% beers really kick in late in the evening. We had enough sense to start our way home, but we got side tracked when we noticed an interesting little place on a forked intersection.

We make our way into the bar to see what beers are offered on tap. The place isn't fancy, but feels comfortable. We notice Kasteel Brune on tap. Always a favorite of ours, we order two and move to a table outside.

Our beer soaked brains began speaking to the guys next to us. Using a little Spanish, a little French, and some English we seem to hit it off. Nina heads into the bar for another round. She asks the bartender if she could pour her own beers. The bartender has no problem with that. In fact he gives her an apron to wear while she's doing it. I think he let her practice on the Maes Pils, a relatively inexpensive beer. After a few tries she pours a couple of perfect glasses.

The bartender then suggests that she deliver the beers to the table. So there she is with a Ciney beer tray, a Grimbergen apron, and two Maes pils. Well, the beers were for the guys at the table next to us, and did they get a laugh when she showed up with the beers, tray, and apron.

Meanwhile, the bartender takes a Kasteel Beer sign off the wall, dusts it off and cleans it up. He presents this to Nina as her graduation certificate of bartending. That was a great finish to a great day.

A visit to Brussels must include a quick stop at a specialty beer store named the BierTemple, located just behind Grand Place on the North side. All kinds of beeraphanalia are to be found here. They also sell lots of beers ready to ship or ready to take to the hotel and drink. It's a tiny place that is packed with all kinds of stuff, and there are always plenty of people wandering through it.

On one visit as I was side stepping past another person, my feet bumped into and clanged some bottles of beer together that were sitting on the floor. I checked them out and noticed no labels on the beer bottles. My pulse quickened. My first thought was that these were bottles of Westvleteren. On closer examination the bottle cap told the story. The caps were in two different colors, red and green, with the famous Trappist abbey name.

These beers are hard, to near, impossible to get. Their website, sintsixtus.be, has some peculiar, but informative, information on just how to go about getting their beer. The abbey brews and sells the beer on irregular schedules and only sells at the abbey. People interested in buying the beer must make an appointment over the phone, drive their cars there and wait on line to get just a limited few. The purchaser must also promise not to resell the beers. This was a rare find indeed. We purchased two bottles to bring back to the hotel with us.

We returned to our favorite Brussels hotel, the Hotel Mozart with our two Westvleteren beers and a chunk of Belgian cheese we picked up from a local cheese shop. The hotel has a tiny courtyard with a couple of tables. We popped open the beers and cut up the cheese. The beers had many flavors going on, and although freshly brewed they somehow seemed already aged. A thick cream-colored head that stood up till the end, the beer was almost chewy.

Those Trappist Monks really know what they are doing. This combination made for a heavenly afternoon happy hour.

One of my favorite things about Travels for Beer is to sit in an outdoor café, sip on a delicious beer, people watch and talk about the scene around me with Nina.

On this particular day, it was a late afternoon in Brussels, Belgium. It was a sunny Fall day with the temperature in the mid 50's. The kind of day where a sweater or sweatshirt warms you up, but your beer does not overheat in the sun. Our Belgian ales were at a perfect 55 degrees.

Nina was probably drinking a Kasteel Brune, one of her favorites here, and hard to find at home. It is 11%, sweet and malty. I was probably drinking a Rochefort 12. Dark, delicious with hints of raisins. We've got our feet up on the chairs across from us, our sunglasses on, and wondering if it gets any better than this!

Our café is at a busy pedestrian intersection across from a park on one side and an entrance to a shopping plaza on the other side. Foot traffic is busy on both sides of the cobbled street. Grand Place, the very old and ornate plaza, is behind us about 100 meters. We imagine everyone is either sitting have a beer, coming from just having a beer, or on their way to having a beer. We can hear music playing in the park. No one is inside the café on this wonderful day. Gare Midi is nearby so people are trailing luggage behind them as they pass by us both to and from the station.

Across from us and to one side of us are ice cream stands. They are both doing a brisk business. There are two cafés beside ours, one serving coffee and the other beer. Nina and I figure that here in Brussels you either have a beer, a coffee and pastry, or ice cream. All of the cafes are filled with people. We are tourists, so we order some moules, or mussels, to pair with our beers.

The people walking by seem to be at a slower pace than what I am use to seeing at home. That is to say if I do see people walking. Of course walking is still a major mode of transportation in a large city, but elsewhere it seems to not exist. I like to walk in my town in Florida and never seem to pass anyone else on the sidewalk. When I do reach my destination, hedges or lawns sometimes block access from the sidewalk to the front door. However, here everyone is moving slow, going nowhere in particular, as if they were doing laps around the city.

Some people are on their mobile, some people walk with their arms behind their backs, some are pushing carriages and some are walking hand in hand with another. Just walking, somewhere. The café is filled with people of all types. There are students with backpacks, tourists with maps, singles reading a newspaper, and couples enjoying conversation.

Nina and I notice two elderly women approaching from one end of our street. They are only 30 meters away, but at their rate they are several minutes from passing in front of us. They are either sisters or best friends. They both carry canes in one hand. The arms that touch while walking side by side are used for support. They each have a purse draped over their forearm. It is a little chilly for them so they wear their hats and a jacket. They never stop their conversation while remaining vigilant on the rough cobblestones in the street.

While Nina and I watch, we get refills on our beers. The elderly ladies are still passing by. Then, they both raise their heads up from the street and with a smile, turn up our row of tables at the café. They sit at the table just in front of us.

They did have a destination after all. They put their canes down and loosened their collars. A few words are exchanged with the waiter and and off he goes. Nina and I wonder what they will be having this sunny day. To our surprise the waiter returns with two bottles of Duvel and two of their signature tulip shaped glasses.

Bravo for them! Sante! They pour their beers like champs and seem very satisfied with their choices. We can be sure that they have done this before. How many times? By this time Nina and I have ordered some cheese to go with our new round of beers. Triple Karmeliet for me and Duvel for Nina.

I wish that I had gone over and spoken with the ladies. Just imagine the stories they could tell us. However, we thought it would be a little inappropriate to intrude their space. Nina was guessing at their backgrounds and their conversation. It would be great to buy them some moules or another Duvel and sit back and listen to their tales.

But, we didn't speak with them. They finished their golden beers with the large white foamy top in no rush. They were then on their way again.

We don't know where they were going, and we didn't get their email addresses! But I think it was better this way, with just our own imaginative stories.

ANTWERP

With a population of 750,000, Antwerpen has been a major port city since the 14th Century. Located on the Schelde River, it's Grote Markt rivals Brussel's Grand Place. The Guild Houses have been restored to their 16th Century brilliance.

Sometimes all this beer hunting and research work is exhausting. You can't be in a pub or tavern every minute of every day of your trip. Sightseeing is a must. The perfect balance must be achieved. The beer and the pubs are better understood if you understand the people and the area. Sightsee a little bit, sighttaste a little bit. (I think I just coined a new word; sighttaste.)

Anyway, Nina and I are in Antwerp the diamond city of Belgium and one of the top areas of the world in the diamond trade. There are great places to visit and shops to tour, which are involved with the marketing and cutting of diamonds. It's a good way to stay dry on a rainy day.

Our rainy day involved a trip to the Antwerp Zoo. Great show, just behind the main train station. They have a pair of rare white rhinos, and a great variety of other animals including lions, tigers, giraffes, elephants, and a large assortment of monkeys. The monkeys here are different than the monkeys in the pubs.

When it comes time for lunch Nina and I decide to check out the cafeteria. It smells good and the food looks good so we grab a tray. This cold rainy day requires hot soup and a good dark bread. No problem here. We slide our tray down the line to the beverage area and check out the offerings. The usual sodas and juices and, what is that brown bottle proudly standing in the refrigerator?

It's Westmalle dubbel! Wow, we can hardly believe our eyes. One beer offered on this cafeteria line and it is one of the hardest beers to find in a good liquor store at home in the USA. If we were at a zoo in the States, first, beer most likely would not be offered, and second, if beer were offered, it would be one of those mass-produced tasteless types. But not here. As I have said before, the beer is not frowned upon but it is revered. Beer is accepted as part of their lives and is respected.

Nina and I just had to laugh. Our time at the zoo was supposed to be our time off from our "work". We could not get away from it. Okay, we'll have two Westmalle with our soup and bread. Cost us a fortune also, almost $3 a bottle! We were so excited and surprised that we actually took photos of ourselves drinking our Westmalle and eating our lunch at the zoo. With the hot soup in our stomachs and the tasty Westmalle finished, we moved on to see the monkeys. They were quite entertaining that afternoon.

That evening we were ready to seek out our destination bar in Antwerpen named the Kulminator. The Kulminator is renown amongst the Beer Travelers as a great beer bar and a not to miss site. I first found out about it from *All About Beer* Magazine in one of their travels articles and before that a mention from Michael Jackson. It is located at Vleminckveld, 32.

The bar was located about a 20-minute walk South of the main square, which made for a 40-minute walk for us from our hotel. Our map was not the best, but we had an exact address. We walked and walked. All the turns and intersections that we passed through matched our non-detailed map.

Finding the exact address seemed to be troublesome for us. We needed to do some backtracking and extra walking but finally came across the location on a side street. The pub is clearly marked with a large vertical reading sign, some hops hanging over the door, and two large billboards to each side of the door proclaiming something in Dutch. The words that I think I can translate are "beer specialists in beer specialties". We're happy to reach our destination.

We grasp the doorknob in anticipation of trying some good beers. We find the door locked! Could it be closed on this Monday evening? Nina jiggles the door, but it is not opening. Did we walk all this way for disappointment? We almost walk away frustrated but try the door one more time and it opens. We walk into a dimly lit, long and narrow room. Plenty of wood and lots of beer signs covering the walls and the tabletops. The bar with ten bar stools, is on the left. It has leaded glass storage cabinets built above. Classical music is playing in the air. One sole customer sitting at the bar reading and sipping a beer.

We notice an elderly gent behind the bar who reminds me of the crazy professor from the movie *Back to the Future*, and an elderly lady working the tables. There are only about a dozen tables placed on two slightly different levels. We grab a table and start to look over all the stuff on the table. What should we eat and what should we drink? The beer menu is extensive, but I concentrate on the draft beer selections.

We order Kasteel Brune and Gordon's Scotch Ale, which are both on tap, and a plate of smoked sausage, cheese, and olives to go with the beers. We look around and notice lots of advertising on the walls for beer. Hops are hanging from the ceiling and flowers are on the tables. The classical music playing is very peaceful and contenting to be drinking the beers brewed by monks. Sitting on the bar is a very large book, the size of a large, antique, family Bible. Nina checks it out and finds that it is the beer list!

We have learned that the Kulminator is famous for it's collection of vintage beers. But that list is more than what we expected. Of course, you can order a bottle of Chimay Blue here, but you can order your Chimay by the year. This is a rare collection indeed.

The simple food menu is perfect for tasting beers. Our snack plate is delivered with a small bowl of olives, a cutting board and knife for the cheese and salami. This simple snack is just what we love with our beers. The Gordon's Scotch ale is a pretty brown red color, 8.6%, a tad smoky, fruity, and very tasty. It was served with the most unusual shaped glass that I have seen. I understand the shape of the glass enhances the taste of the beer and this glass shape was really thought out. It had a triangular or funnel like top sitting above a bowl like bottom, which again was sitting upon a short stem. Nina always loves her

Kasteel brown when we are able to find it on tap. It's a high potency beer with terrific fruit and chocolate flavors.

Two guys enter the bar and add a little life to the atmosphere. They seem to know the lady working the tables, regular customers we guess. Quickly a few more gents enter and there are five young guys in their twentys sitting at the table next to us. It seems to be a party of some sort. They have a variety of great beers in front of them.

Nina and I select Bruges Triple and Golden Draak for our second tasting. The Golden Draak is an Antwerpen beer named after a golden statue on top of the clock tower in Ghent, it's 10.5%, dark in color, and has a full body. The Bruges Triple is a 9% wheat beer from a little town in the Western part of Belgium named Bruges. Bruges is a great brewing city that deserves a few days of tasting.

We love the service here. So many different types of beer were ordered, always served with the perfectly shaped glass with a logo, and always with the slow, perfect pour.

Nina is in one of her socializing moods and decides to start a conversation with the guys. She finds out that they are celebrating two birthdays. About half of them speak or understand English. There always seems to be one person friendlier than the others, or at least more curious than the others. We meet Egon, one of the birthday boys, and ask and answer questions of each other.

Soon, we know everyone's name and we are raising our glasses of perfect beer to toast each other. Schkole! We slide over to their table and join in with the party. They find out that we are beer lovers and they want to buy us a beer that we have never had. Well, that is not easy to do, but if it is going to happen this is the best place. They suggest a few beer names to me and I shake my head several times, nope I've had that. Then finally they suggest Westvleteren, the Trappist beer that is hard to find anywhere. I happily accept their offering.

Remember, Westvleteren can only be purchased at the monastery through a reservation phoned in ahead. The purchaser must also promise not to resell the beer. So the owners here are going to break a little rule, but at least I get to experience the beer.

They even have promotional material on the tables for the beer. How rare is that stuff? The table tent had a sticker on it reading "niet meenemen a.u.b." which translates in English to read "please don't take away" information about beer, is also interesting for other beer lovers! I'm embarrassed to say, that, the table tent now sits on my home bar top.

Even walking to the bathroom is a sightseeing tour. As you walk to the rear of the pub you will pass a room with a large window to peer into. The room is a cooled cellaring area for aging the beers. It seems organized with boxes and bottles of all types of beers.

Upon reaching the men's room, I quickly notice that the hardware on the hand wash sink is a tap handle for the faucet and a keg spigot for the spout. I can't get away from the beer atmosphere here!

Returning from the toilet, I see a long gray haired gent with a guitar standing at our table. It seems he has found our birthday party and wants to know if it would be acceptable for him to play us some music. Of course!

Nina and I needed to return the favor of the bought drinks. We wanted to taste the different years of Chimay side by side. There are seven of us. Oh, what the hell, let's order seven years worth. We start with 1985 and end with 1991. Some of the Chimay labels had the year printed on them, and the earlier years did not. The owner had a hand written sticker indicating the year attached to the bottle.

So we start the tasting. We open each bottle and pour it in a glass. We then pass the glass around and each person takes a sip. We all quickly realize that to be fair, we must start the newly poured glass with a different person with each new beer. Now, that is a bunch of friendly drunks thinking at their best and fairest. Here we are sharing a glass with seven strangers, but being fair about it by allowing a different person to be the first person to drink from the glass before it is passed around the table. We figured this process out from the very first Chimay! Why can't governments of the world be this democratic in solving the world's problems? Let them drink beer!

We were so conscientious about this tasting we even kept tasting notes. In the end of this glorious tasting, it was surprising that we reached a unanimous consensus that the 1985 was the best year. Amazing, a group of seven strangers has just agreed on which of seven beers was most pleasing to the palate. The power of beer. Nina's notes on the 1985 are "it has a rich, blackberry, currant taste, it's delicious".

By now, it was getting late, and many of our new friends had to go to work in the morning. We were surprised to find out that all except one, had either walked or rode a bicycle to the Kulminator. The people of Europe are very serious about not drinking and driving, with stiff penalties.

Our Belgian hosts were quite insistent that we not walk back to the hotel. The one guy who had driven to the bar had already left for home. Someone grabbed a cell phone and he was called back to give us a ride. He came back to the bar, picked us up and drove us to the hotel across town. I felt safe with him driving because he was really very careful with his beer consumption during our tasting session.

Schkole! Happy Birthday to Egon and Wim! Hello to Geert, Koen, Ebert, and Koen. Nina was given the nickname Nina Beer when they understood my nickname was Bill Boli. Boli is short for stromboli, the famous sandwich served at Stuff Yer Face. She also coined a new word "bluzzy" when she was taking a picture of the beer Bible. She said the photo was bluzzy, a cross between blurry and fuzzy! It was a great night out for Nina and I. Congratulations to the Kulminator for being one of the best beer bars in the world.

The Kulminator opened in 1978 and is owned by Dirk Van Dyck and Leen Boudewijn, who were married in 1973.

GHENT

While staying in Brussels, we made a day trip to the city of Ghent. It was about a 45-minute train ride to the West of Brussels. Ghent has a population of about 250,000 who are Flemish speaking and of an independent mind. The earlier residents sided with the English against the French in the 1700's.

It is a long walk from the train station to the old town area, but definitely worth the trek. This area is very impressive with its large stone buildings and cobblestone streets that are crossed several times by the meandering Leie River. An occasional cable car will drive by. The 360-degree views from the stone bridge of St. Michaels are to be remembered. So many towers, belfrys and castles pierce the sky. Our day had a clear blue sky.

There is a castle with a large moat at a high point in the city that we visited, named The Gravensteen, or Castle of the Counts of Flanders. There we visited the torture chambers. The churches of the city are several hundred years old and beautiful.

We stopped for a bier at a riverside outdoor café, de Grill Restaurant. The proprietor was just opening up on this sunny morning and he politely brought us a table outside. From our vantage point we could clearly see Saint Jacobs church tower rising above the city and the river. I enjoyed a Jan van Gent from Liefman's brewing. Liefman's brews naturally fermented beers in open tanks. It's 5.5%, light and cloudy, with hints of fruit. The bottle was wrapped in some classy blue foil.

A little more walking around and a late lunch stop at Waterhuis de Bierkant along the waterfront. The place looks great from the bridge crossing the river to it and is very inviting. We were not disappointed. The menu lists 150 beers with 14 on tap. The interior has brick walls and hops are hanging from the ceiling. Jazz and blues are playing in the background. The bar is also made from old brick. The staff was very friendly and welcoming. From the beer list I notice that they stock Aachel, the last of the seven Trappist beers that I have not yet been able to taste. I order up the #8. It has a nice brown color, 8% alcohol, delicious, but not as tasty as my favorite Westmalle dubbel.

The food menu was beer friendly, listing items cooked with beer. We wanted to order lunch, but we were told that the kitchen was closed for lunch. We must have looked disappointed because the server grabbed our stuff and moved us next door to Eethuisje Chez Leontine, which was a sister restaurant.

One of the items on the menu was rabbit braised with Chimay Premiere. We selected for our lunch, Ghent stew made with beef stewed in Westmalle and Rodenbach beers served with frites. This was absolutely delicious! I wish I could have stayed here all day and then eaten dinner here also.

We needed to leave picturesque Ghent to catch a train back to Brussels and had the long walk back to the train station. Along the way though we passed what we thought was the smallest free standing bar we had ever seen, 't Galgen Huisje, which means gallows house. Built in the 17th century it stood by itself on a small square and looked like a two story dollhouse. It could not have been more than 12 feet square with an attic and a pitched ceiling. We sat upstairs at a tiny table along side a picture window to the square. Great place to people watch, and they could just as easy watch you in the window. We looked llike a scene out of *Alice in Wonderland*.

We headed back to the train station and followed a route along a narrow river. The shore of the river was lined with boats, which seemed to be lived on by their owners. Very interesting. We came across one boat that had a neon sign on it announcing "bar open". We didn't think he was just a cool guy, but that it was really an open bar. He was selling drinks! We're not sure of the laws here, but he seemed open for business. Nina and I hate to pass up an opportunity like that, but we had to catch a train. Can you imagine the stories we would have heard from that guy?

About 100 feet further down the river from the houseboat bar we came across a funny site. Right along side the pathway was a shiny stainless steel public pissort. It reminded me of a cartoon of someone standing with a barrel around his or her body. A person could walk into this steel barrel, do his business, and watch the world go by at the same time. It was a good relief spot and a great photo opportunity.

Our visit to Ghent was too quick. It deserves at least one night and two days. We'll be back for another visit.

We will also be back to Belgium for another visit. I have finally had the opportunity to taste each of the Trappist ales, and they never fail to satisfy. There is always a wow factor within the bottle. Besides the Trappist beers, there are hundreds of other Belgian beers to taste crossing a wide spectrum of styles. Many small breweries are open to tours and tastings. Search the web and you can find a beer festival several times during the year. The range of flavors, styles and strengths of the beers is mind boggling, so we'll take it one beer at a time.

LA TRAPPE
ABBEY DE KONINGSHOEVEN, NETHERLANDS

Although the abbey is located across the border from Belgium in the Netherlands, I will include the story of our visit here. The abbey is over 120 years old, and the monks have been brewing since 1894. It is the only Trappist beer to be brewed outside of Belgium.

The twin towers of Abbey of Our Lady of Koningshoeven are located just outside of the city Tilburg. Nina and I based ourselves in Eindhoeven, Netherlands for two nights. We arrive at our hotel early in the afternoon and quickly got on a train to Tilburg. The train ride was probably only about an hour long. Once in Tilburg we needed to figure out the bus routes and take a bus to the abbey. We waited almost an hour for our bus to depart. Our directions weren't exact, but we knew this bus would pass by the abbey at some point. I just wasn't sure when and just where it was.

After about fifteen minutes on the bus, I spotted a sign for the abbey on the roadside, and Nina and I jumped off the bus. We quickly realize that it was just a sign with the abbey name and an arrow pointing straight ahead. So we start walking on this drizzly gray day and follow the sign. The road winds through the countryside, dotted with small homes. We soon cross a small river and a bridge. The road opens up to some open fields and the road is lined with tall full trees for almost a mile. It was beautiful!

We are a little worried that we may not be going in the right direction. I step from underneath the hanging branches of the trees and step into the open field. Off in the distance I can see tall towers that look like they belong to an abbey. This must be the right direction. The walk on the road was a bit dangerous because there was no sidewalk, and the autos were speeding by on this straight away.

Nevertheless, we were on our pilgrimage to the Trappist beers of Koningshoeven, and we felt protected.

Soon we approached the gated entrance to the abbey. One of the first things we notice is a bus stop sign and covered area. If we had been patient, our bus would have dropped us off right in front of the abbey. Little did we know. I suppose, we were anxious.

The abbey has an attached gift shop and a beer tasting room. It was late in the afternoon, almost five o'clock. We had spent so much time traveling and locating this place, and now we are worried that it may be closing! We walk into the tasting room and are correct that it is closing in fifteen minutes. We are the only customers present. It is not a large room, but comfortable with wooden tables and walls decorated with La Trappe signage. The bar is front and center with walk up service. The blonde, dubbel, triple, and quadruple are flowing from the tap.

We quickly remove our coats, grab a table, and walk up to the bar. A friendly member of the staff greets us, and she explains that there are tasting sizes of each beer or full pours of each available. Since our time is so limited, we decide to go with the tasting size of each. The beers were inexpensive. Our happy bartender then tells us not to rush, enjoy the beers. We do just that. We got four samples, one each of the blonde, dubbel, triple, and quadruple. Each looked so beautiful, each served in miniature, goblet style glass.

The beers were very delicious, but four ounces of each was not going to satisfy the two of us. We noticed a food menu written on a blackboard mounted to the wall. It included some of our favorites of cheese, breads, sausages, and soups. Is it really closing time? Did we really blow it? We notice that the bartender is talking and laughing with what seems to be some other employees, and not in a hurry to clean up and leave.

I try for another beer. No problem, I grab two for us. It's past closing time, but it's not a problem. A half hour goes by and we try to get two more beers. The bartender is not available so a gentleman in a blue jump suit with the La Trappe logo on it pours us two beers. He speaks English. We tell him our story and thank him for serving us a couple of beers past the closing hour. We find out that he is the brewer here!

Nina and I dazzle Ludwig, the brewer, with our beer knowledge and find ourselves in a good beer conversation with him. Soon his beer is empty and he offers to fill us up again. He explains that it is his recipe for the special Bock beer of the season this year, and has a few extra bottles left over. It seems that the Bock should only be sold until the start of June, and it was June 1. This year's bock had been stored for two years. It was delicious, smooth, and almost velvety. It was an honor to be drinking this beer with the brewer.

We had an interesting conversation with Ludwig. He told us that the monks do work the bottling line, but do not like to work with the regular workers. About ten of them actually put some time in during the process. I mentioned to him that I was surprised that the beers were on tap. Most often the Trappist beers are only bottled. He explained that the recipe is slightly different for the bottles than the kegs. The bottled beer is conditioned with an extra amount of sugar and yeast before bottling, while the kegs are not.

I asked why the La Trappe beers are sold under the name of Koningshoeven in the USA. He explained that the monks thought the name, La Trappe, was too similar to the name of their order, the Trappists, which may bring confusion to the other six Trappist beers. It was now getting late, and Ludwig suggested we return tomorrow for a personal tour of the brewery. Okay with us!

Eindehoven was a good choice for a place to spend our night. There is a terrific old town area. I'm not too sure what is actually old or what is rebuilt, but either way there were some very nice bars to visit.

Eindehoven played a major role during World War II. Soon after the Allies had landed in Normandy and started their trek across France, they realized they needed a way to make a major hit on the Nazi's to gain control and bring about victory quickly. Their idea was to drop thousands of paratroopers behind enemy lines and sweep around the front lines and into Germany. Eindhoven was in the center of this offensive, of which its outcome was not very successful.

The next morning we get on a 9:30 express train to Tilburg. We are anticipating the brewery tour and lunch in the tasting room. We again get on our bus, and this time stay on until the bus pulls perfectly up in front of the abbey. Total trip time was less than an hour and a half this second visit. Again, it is a drizzly day and colder than yesterday. The gift shop and tasting room don't open for another thirty minutes.

We are standing in the parking lot and admiring the surroundings. A car or a truck occasionally whizzes by on the tree-lined road passing alongside the abbey. Then we notice a large group of bicycles approaching, around the distant bend in the road. We are a little surprised, but in the Netherlands, it seems the bicycle is a major form of transportation. The railway stations are jammed with literally thousands of bikes parked.

As this group of about 30 cyclists approaches us, they turn into the parking lot of the abbey. The group is made up entirely of women, all probably in the sixty to seventy age group. Nina and I always laugh that when we are out at the pubs during our travels we seem to meet groups of men, and never any women. I would pray for meeting some women. Well, this time is different! We will get to party with the women. However, I forgot to specify young women in my prayer. They park their bikes outside the tasting room, and it is now opening time.

Nina and I get our first beers before the large group does. We watch them order, and we are disappointed that they all get coffee, except for one of them. There is no party today. We take some photos, them of us, and us of them. Soon Ludwig arrives and waives us to come outside with him. He seems to be in a hurry.

He has promised us a tour, but he is short handed in the brewery today, so we must hurry. We are just happy to be getting the tour. We pass through a gate and enter a wooden door in an old brick building. The smell inside is wonderful, filled with aromas of hops and malt. The warmth of the room also feels good on this cold dreary morning. Ludwig quickly shows us all around. We take a few photos. Then Ludwig, as if remembering something, looks at his watch and runs off in another direction. He mutters something about the brew batch. Nina and I are left alone in the brew house. We wonder, should we help ourselves to a taste?

Very shortly, Ludwig returns and explains that he is in the middle of something and must say goodbye to us. Politely, he mentions for us to find our own way out. Okay. For that one quick instant, I felt like we were in charge of the beer. But, it didn't last long. We climbed some metal stairs and found our way out, and across the grounds and back to the tasting room. Our group of cyclist friends was gone, but it was time for lunch and more tasting.

La Trappe brews five different beers regularly. The blonde is gold in color, the lightest tasting and 6.5%. The dubbel, is ruby red in color, has a soft mouth feel, very fragrant, and 7%. The Triple is dark colored, 8%, fruity and bittersweet. The Quadrupel is 10%, full flavored but still retains a soft mouth feel. A witte, or wheat, is also brewed that we did not taste. All of the beers are delicious, and are easiest to compare when they are drank side by side. The food menu has all of the essentials to accompany the beers.

A visit to the gift shop is a good idea after the beer tasting. As a reminder, the proceeds go to a charity. You can purchase bottles of the beers and many items with the La Trappe logo on it. We purchased a .75 liter bottle of Quadrupel to bring home and cellar for a special occasion. It was a great stop at La Trappe.

Remember, to taste the La Trappe beers here in the USA, look for the Koningshoeven label.

THE PACIFIC NORTHWEST, USA

Nina and I are on our way to Portland, Oregon and Seattle, Washington. It's about two and a half hours from West Palm Beach, Florida to Houston where we change planes and then another four and a half hours to Portland, Beervana. The flight time is nearly the same for a trip to England and just less than the time needed to reach central Europe.

We are a little anxious of the destination we have selected because we do love our visits to Europe. However, we are anticipating some great beer diversity in Portland and Seattle. In that way, it will be very different than in Europe. When you step into a Brauhaus in Germany usually the selection of beer styles is limited to two or four. In Cologne, it is almost completely limited to one style. Drinking in Brussels is an adventure for the taste buds where each sip of the brown and gold ales has various flavors to visit. We don't expect any new styles of beer to taste here in the Northwest, but we do expect great examples of old familiar styles. This is where the craft brewing sensation has reached a pinnacle of success, and that is why it is known as Beervana.

Of course, we have done our homework and are armed with a list of brewpubs for each city along with maps and suggested pub-crawls. It looks as if we have a lot of work to do. Two websites really help us with the maps and lists, the Oregon Brewers Guild site at oregonbeer.org and The Washington Brewers Guild site at washingtonbeer.com.

I've heard a lot about the Pacific Northwest in the United States, and my research before embarking on the next travels for beer confirms some rumors that I have read.

The Oregon Brewers Guild really has it together on their website. You can order, free, a four-color brochure with beer information and a map of their brewpubs and microbreweries. The brochure mentions that Oregon has 60 brewing companies operating 80 facilities. Portland alone has 30 breweries within its city limits, proclaiming "more than any other city in the world". I checked Wikipedia and found out that Portland has a population of 556,000. If they have 30 breweries, that is one brewery for every 18,500 people. That is one brewery for every man and woman, child or senior citizen. That is pretty good. That's a place you can quench your thirst! Oregon has earned the nicknames "Beervana" and "Brewtopia".

On the Washington Brewers Guild web site, they state their mission to "advance their common interests and promote the quality and value of their beers". They state the number of breweries as either 80 or 82 within the state (I found both numbers on the web site). I counted 19 within the city limits of Seattle on their map. The list of brewpubs in Seattle is conveniently detailed with the bus routes and stops to help you find each and every one of them!

Washington is also number one in the United States for growing hops. According to the Washington Hop Commission, the state had a yield of about 52 million pounds in 2000, which is 77% of the total US production and 25% of the world production. Oregon yielded less hops, at eight million pounds, and ranked second in the US according to the Oregon Hops Commission.

After about ten hours of actual airport and flight time, we arrive at Portland's airport. It is located about 15 miles to the Northeast of the city center. We get our first glimpse of the Portland lifestyle when we find out that the train to the downtown area costs only two dollars each, and it is clean and on time. The light rail train drops us off about four blocks from our hotel. The staff at the hotel is friendly and asks us about our visit. We mention that we are here to taste the great beers of Portland. He laughs, grabs a map from behind the desk and quickly marks an X to indicate the location of Henry's 12th Street Tavern. It is not a brewpub but they have about 50 beers on tap from the area. He mentions to us that he was there all of last night.

Sounds like a great place for us to start. It is late afternoon and we haven't had lunch yet. We're thirsty and we're hungry. Let's drop off the bags and get to it. Henry's was comfortable, airy, and bright with a large circular bar with all the taps working their way around the inside of the bar. The building is a renovation of an old Weinhard Brewery. Weinhard was the first brewery in Portland, which opened in 1852. The food menu has many creative ideas and some of the old standbys. The majority of the beer list consists of craft beers from Colorado and West to California along with some old European classics.

Our bartender was friendly and ready to point us in the right direction for our beer tastings. My first choice was from Big Sky Brewing in Montana, Moose Drool, a dark brown ale that was smooth and malty. It went down very quickly and appeasing. Nina's first beer was from Anderson Valley Brewing in California, the Winter Solstice. An amber colored seasonal beer slightly sweet, bubbly, and a full malty texture.

Nina and I were reading the menus and notice a happy hour menu that starts at 3pm. It seemed to us that the prices were almost ridiculously inexpensive. Mac N Chez is only $1.95, crab cakes are $3.95 and a steak sandwich is $3.95. We were a few minutes early for that so we ordered lunch from the regular menu. Great food.

My second beer at Henry's was from Amnesia Brewing Co. located in Portland. An IPA named Desolation, which was light, fresh, and hoppy with a nice brown color. If this was an indication of the taste of Portland's beers, I was ready for more. Nina switched to another seasonal, Deschutes Jubelale. Deschutes is one of the larger brewers in the area. The Jubelale was amber in color and reminded us of a hoppy stout. A little too potent for Nina so we shared it. This was our first indication that the beers here in the Northwest were going to be big in flavor. Big in hops and big in malt.

With some food in our stomachs, we ventured out into the streets with our map in hand. With a short walk North we came across a Rogue Ale House. No brewing here, but they must have had 15 different Rogue beers on tap to taste. This was a good opportunity for us, because on the East Coast we can usually only purchase Rogue beers in 22 ounce bottles. That size is just a little too large for first tastings, and I can't carry them in my bar because it prices out to high.

The bartender was almost too friendly, but quick to offer any three-ounce tasting that we desired. Nina likes to taste before buying a full pint. I know by experience, I can usually finish a pint of anything. How risky could it be ordering a beer in Portland? I go for the Chipotle ale. I've seen the beer around on shelves at home, but never was inclined to purchase it. This was the perfect place to give it a go. Of course, the first flavor to hit the tongue is the smokiness. Not over whelming, subtle, but I was tired of the smoke about half way through the beer.

This is when I realized that maybe I just enjoy the classic flavors of beer. You know, the German Reinheitsgebot Law of 1518 that states you can use nothing other than water, malt, hops and yeast to brew a beer. No fruit flavors, no spices, just well balanced between the malt and hops. The same for the atmosphere of a bar, not too cute or perky or branded, just the basics.

Nina continued with the free tastings. She liked the Uber Pils. Fresh hops, but subtle on the taste buds. Nice white head. Nina notices that one of the many taps is a Guinness. What? We ask the bartender why and he smiles while telling us if it ain't broken don't fix it. He's got a point. I then notice a little thin silver beer handle. It looks familiar to me. No, it can't be. Is that the Silver Bullet? Sheepishly the bartender tells us that sometimes you just have to go with something mainstream for the public. I didn't think it was possible out here in Beervana to see a Coors light tap handle. Little did we know it would be the last time.

We're tired from our trip out here, plus we only had four hours of sleep before our long flight. We start walking back to the hotel and spot a dimly lit neon sign jutting out from the façade of another pub. Well, one more before we retire for the night.

We've come across Tugboat Brewing Co. On the wall Tugboats are described as small, powerful and hardworking. Just like their beers I suppose. Another friendly bartender, quick to hand out the samples. I think Nina likes it here because she could enjoy just the samples alone. She's not afraid to ask for two or three, or maybe four samples, before deciding on her pint of choice. I order the Tugboat ESB, which again is fresh tasting, hoppy and amber in color. Nina orders the amber ale. Basic beer flavors. The amber ale is darker than the ESB and hoppy. I'm not sure if it's because we are tired, but we both agree that we are tired of the hops, already. "Stop the hops!" These two examples of different beer styles, taste about the same to us. Hoppy. We even do a blind tasting and can't tell the difference. Maybe we're getting cranky. Two pints for only $5. I guess the hops are cheap around here. We leave half the beers and head on home to rest up for tomorrow's tastings.

The Willamette River runs North and South through Portland, and the Columbia River is on its Northern side running East and West. The Willamette has several bridges crossing it, and a park on the West side named after a former Governor, Tom McCall. Nina and I walk North from the hotel to verify the location of the Amtrak train station that we'll be using on Sunday morning. From there we head to the river, follow the path along its West side, and follow it South. There are many people running, walking, riding bicycles and just sitting reading papers. Portland is also a great bicycle city with bike lanes everywhere. I've noticed plenty of commuters riding bikes.

The Fall weather is to our liking. Nina from the desert of Las Vegas doesn't get to see the leaves change color often, and me, with spending the last three years in Florida, misses it. It's a little foggy this morning and the colors of the leaves are just brilliant. It's a photo opportunity of course.

Eventually we wind our way down to the Southern end of the city's core and find ourselves in front of a beautiful woodsy restaurant named McCormick & Schmick's. A restaurant chain founded in Seattle, I'm familiar with the name because there are some units on the East Coast. More importantly, Full Sail Brewing has set their tanks up inside to brew some beers on premise. It's just about 11 am, a little bit early, but we quit early last night so we need to start early today!

We step inside to a beautiful place, wood and brass galore, and a fantastic view over the Willamette. The early sun was twinkling off the recently polished brass beer taps. I think we'll stay here for a while. Nina and I are excited and pull up the best bar stools in the place because we're the first to arrive. Of course, a friendly bartender greets us. Seems that's normal here in Portland. Jordan was our bartender.

My first beer out of the shoot or "out of the cask" was the cask conditioned amber ale. Jordan asked me if I would like my glass cold from the fridge or at room temperature! Wow, that's good. I never had that question asked of me before. I prefer room temperature over a cold glass, as it allows you to better taste the flavors of the beer. The amber ale was just delicious, a perfect balance of hops and malt.

Nina was a happy camper because they sell their beers by a group tasting. Seven in all, with about four ounces of each of amber ale, pale ale, IPA, Winter ale Wassail, Lupeller, stout, and Belgian style gold. I remind her to look, smell, taste, note the mouth feel and the finish of each beer. Nina is good with her tasting notes and makes notes in our logbook. On the pale ale she notes that it would be a good "session" beer. The Lupeller seems to be her favorite with notes of, rich and delicious, spicy, warm, orangy and hoppy. The Belgian style reminded her of a Duvel, but slightly over done on the sweetness of the coriander.

I continued with tasting the three beers direct from the cask. After the amber ale warm up I moved on to the cask Lupeller. We noted that the cask Lupeller was cloudy compared to Nina's keg Lupeller, and the taste was more rounded from the cask. The Brewmaster here is John Harris, president of the Brewers Guild. He definitely has some good beers going on.

Full Sail has a slogan that I notice, "Fermenters of Godlike Nectar". I like it. It reminds me of a saying from my college roommate, Bill, who would say "Nectar of the Gods" when talking about his beer. He then added, "If God made anything better, he took it with him!"

The food at the restaurant was also excellent. The menu had salmon prepared many different ways, and all inexpensive. The same inexpensive happy hour menu applies here also. I could get very comfortable in this town. We talk it up with our bartender, Jordan. We tell him we're from Florida and Nina originally from Las Vegas. He wasn't impressed. Usually we're guaranteed that a conversation will start about Las Vegas, but Jordan just began to brag and tell us about Portland. He was born and raised here and wasn't going anywhere. Maybe he's right.

Time to pay the bill. I mention to Nina that I forgot to taste the lager that they had on tap. I find that lagers are rare in a brewpub, I suppose because of the extra time needed to brew and actually store and ferment, or lagern. Surprisingly, Jordan overhears me mention this and brings a Session lager pint along with the check. Now that's service! The lager was terrific, smooth, lively, and just the right amount of hops. Probably like the old brewing days before Prohibition.

Time to leave our great find at Full Sail. Jordan recommends visiting another Full Sail location at the Columbia Gorge. We'll need to rent a car but, it would enable us to stop off and see Multnomah Falls on the way. Sounds like a plan for Saturday. For now, we start walking across the Hawthorne Bridge heading East. Our map tells us that there are several brew pubs on the other side of the river for us to seek out.

There are seven bridges crossing the Wilamette River. Early cities were established along major rivers for many obvious reasons. You see it all across Europe. Just a few blocks across the bridge, we find Roots Brewing. This is an organic brewery. The bar is not open yet, but we wander in. We find the brewer raking the mash out of the kettle. It smells just great here and I think about the lucky pigs that will probably get to eat the spent grains. The brewer is friendly to us (of course, it's Portland), tells us some brewing facts, and invites us back later for a beer. Okay, no problem, we move on.

Just a few blocks further East is Lucky Labrador Brewing Co. It looks like a converted gristmill or barn turned brewery and pub. It's open and somewhat busy for mid afternoon. They serve half pints here, which is great for tasting more styles of beer. The names of two beers grab our attention, Crazy Ludwig Alt and cask Black Lab Stout.

We jump at the Ludwig Alt because we enjoy King Ludwig's castles in Germany and we just visited Dusseldorf the land of alt beers. The alt here is slightly hoppier than we found in Dusseldorf, but it had a good honey amber color. The cask stout was delicious with hints of chocolate and roasted coffee.

While seated there, I noticed single women having lunch, a beer and reading the newspaper. Also a guy dressed in full riding gear rode his bicycle into the pub, leaned it against the wall and ordered a beer at the bar. Seems like a very homey place, appropriate for Portland. Nina notices a sign warning dogs are not allowed inside, but there are photos of dogs everywhere. I guess it is a Health Department thing.

Our fourth stop of the day is Bridgeport Ale House. We are actually heading for Horse Brass Pub, a hike for us, from 10th Street up to 49th. But, that's what we do, walk. If you take a taxi, you might miss something on the way. We didn't miss Bridgeport Ale House though. We stop in and the late Friday afternoon happy hour crowd is starting to build. I have a cask Ropewalk ale. It is very ruby red in color, smooth with a white head. It's refreshing for the hike. $2.50 for a pint! Come on give me a break, "you can't drink gravel water for that price!" Nina goes all the way with a 20-ounce pint of a Belgian Style blond ale named Surpris. It is 6% alcohol, cloudy, and the usual $2.50.

We have the munchies so we sample an appetizer. It's like a small pizza topped with brie cheese, caramelized onions and pears. It's fantastic and goes well with the beers. A perfect match.

Our hike ends at the Horse Brass Pub. It's not a brew pub but an English style pub set in a local residential neighborhood. A sign reads, "If it was anymore authentic, you'd need a passport" and probably an umbrella. They have 50 beers on tap, a full bar, and food menu. It's a little gaudy here with the walls covered with photos, signs and mirrors, but the place is packed and (of course) everyone is friendly. A woman sitting at the next table begins chatting with us immediately and we learn she is also on a pub crawl, with her husband. She points out to us that John Harris is sitting at a table close by. Luckily, we know who Mr. Harris is from our bartender at Full Sail. Remember, he is the brewer at Full Sail and president of the brewer's guild.

I get the chance to have another cask ale, this time Mirror Pond from Deschutes Brewing Co. I remember a Mirror Lake in Alaska and the beautiful reflection of the mountains on the water. The beer is just as beautiful and smooth as the lake, perfectly balanced. Nina drinks the Ebenezer Ale from Bridgeport Ale House. No comments in the log book on the taste of the beer, but she did make note of a little saying she made up on her own "a schnitz for luck and we're on our way". "Schnitz" is a German word we learned in Bamberg, which means a small free amount of beer given to the customer, if asked for, before leaving the pub. Our schnitz was a pint of Hogs Back Stout from the cask brewed by Mt. Hood Brewing that we shared. It was dry, toasty, pleasant, not hoppy, and we liked it better than Guinness. We also shared some sausage here. It wasn't very good, but we ate it, so we must be buzzed from our work.

We decide to get back to our side of town. But it is a long way back, maybe four or six miles. So, we break down and call for the taxi. The cabdriver is shocked we walked here from downtown. We've chosen Bridgeport Brewpub and Bakery for dinner time. That is an unusual combination of a name, but sounds enticing. It was a long cab ride. On the menu, we spot a house made pretzel and order it up. It was not very good, but the ESB mustard was excellent. I ordered the sausage plate but was very disappointed in its flavor. Maybe it was a turkey sausage. Along with the food, I selected a barley wine to drink. Normally a barley wine would be very complex in its flavors, but I found this not to be so. The food menu looks very interesting because they use beer in the flavoring of some of the dishes. We need to come back and give it a second chance.

We decide to end our night (evening) by going to Henry's Tavern on 12th street. Back to basics for me, I order a Pilsner Urquell and Nina orders a Chimay White. These two beers really please our palate and neutralize our taste buds. I can't believe that I ate again by ordering a Mac N Chez with sausage in it! That will get your cholesterol up. However, it was very tasty.

It's 8pm and we're ready to turn into the ever present Fall pumpkin. A good days work. It's a tough job.

We start Saturday by renting a car. Our plan is to drive to Multnomah Falls and then continue East to the city of Hood River and visit Full Sail Brewing. It is suppose to be scenic with a view of the Columbia River. It's only about a 30 mile drive to the falls. When we arrive, it is still foggy in the area. The top of the falls is 620 feet high and we can't see at least half of them. It is a beautiful morning for a hike though. So we get our exercise in for the day and make it up and down the trail. When we return to the bottom the fog has cleared and the sight of the falls is spectacular. It's worth a visit if you are in Portland. One problem, there is no beer here!

Back in the car for another 20 minutes until we reach the city of Hood River. It's a small town and we find Full Sail quickly. When we walk in, I hear an employee state, while giving a small tour of the brewery, that the company is employee owned, the only brewery of its kind. That's a nice twist. I noticed a sign on the wall that reads "specialists in the liquid refreshment arts since 1987". It's just past lunch and the place is busy. Nothing fancy here.

They serve a simple menu along with about eight beers on tap. There is a small outdoor area with ten tables and umbrellas, in addition to the inside room of average size. There are no barstools here. We're lucky enough to grab a table outside with the view of the river and gorge. My first beer is the Imperial Porter. Potent stuff, dark, roasty, with a hint of smoke and nice tan colored head. Nina had the Fall Bock, which was amber in color and smooth. We shared another Mac N Chez, but this time it was something like you made in your college dormitory room. If I wasn't so hungry...

We didn't stay as long here as we thought we would have, before we rented the car. The place just needed more atmosphere, but the beers were good. We decided to just walk the streets of this little town. Surprisingly we came across a brewpub not listed in our guide or shown on the map. We came across Big Horse Ales. Set in the side of a hill, we climbed three flights of stairs to get to the bar area. It is a cozy place with a terrific view of the gorge.

Typically, the bartender was friendly, almost quirky. He knew his beers well, but was thrown out of kilter when a customer ordered a martini. It would throw me off too. Nina's choice of beers was an 8% Scotch ale and I had an Oatmeal stout. Both were full of flavor. The bartender gave us a sample of their pumpkin ale. He was happy to announce that no spices were used in the brew. I was happy to hear that, because sometimes the pumpkin ales are overly spiced with nutmeg and such. This was not, and it was very good with just the hint of the pumpkin flavor.

We don't normally do our bar crawls with a car, so we decide to head on back to Portland while it's safe. It was definitely worth the trip for the scenery and the beers.

When we returned the car to the rental company parking lot, the sun was beginning to go down. We only had a short walk back to the hotel and no plans. We decided to walk a different route to the hotel and came upon an intersection where two streets met at a point. It looked very unusual, but even more unusual was the fact that the sidewalk opened up to a staircase leading down into a small bar. The sign read The Cellar Bar. How clever. We climb down the steep steps and find ourselves in a roughly finished cellar with stone walls, plumbing pipes overhead, electrical wires running along the walls, and a small bar with about eight stools and a dozen tables in the room. A very funky place.

The McMenamin Brothers owned the Cellar Bar. The brothers started in 1983 and now their "Kingdom of Fun" includes about 50 beer bars, unique hotels, pub theaters, and brewpubs in the Northwest. We realize that Halloween will be celebrated here tonight, and this place will be packed later in the night. We stay for one beer each. I enjoyed a Hammerhead pale ale which was a little sweet with an orange/red color. Nina had a Terminator, which was dark and flavorful without being over hopped.

Nina and I are not in the typical Halloween mood, so tonight we'll clean ourselves up and eat at Huber's, the oldest restaurant in Portland, and maybe have some wine for a change. I'll bet we'll have salmon for dinner!

Sunday morning brings our travel day. We need to catch the Amtrak Cascades at 8:45 am for a three-hour ride to Seattle. Portland was a great city. It has a convenient layout, friendly people, and lots of parks, bicycle friendly and great beer and food. All the staff members of the pubs that we visited were knowledgeable about beer. We might be back sooner than we thought.

We're greeted on the train with some comedic employees. The welcome speech over the public address system was a comedy routine to get across the safety issues, ticket process and route to be covered. Seemed odd enough but not for Portland. Tell me I'm crazy, but once settled into my seat and the train on it's way I had a desire for hops. Off to the bistro car to see what beers they may have.

If I were to travel on a train on the East Coast, purchasing a beer would be highly irregular, and if it was even possible, my guess would be that it would be one of those mass produced American beers. The Bistro car, which was rolling down the tracks to Seattle, offered three beers, Pyramid Thunderhead IPA, Pyramid Hefeweizen, and Black Butte Porter! Give me a break...somebody actually planned a well-balanced beer list on this train? Impressive. Reminds me of traveling through Europe on trains where the food served is delicious and the beers well matched. I savored the Pyramid IPA as I watched the scenery roll by the windows. The bottle label read "bursting with hops". It was 6.7% alcohol, smooth, with good well-rounded flavor.

Taking the train instead of driving the 150 miles North was a good idea. The route was very scenic and it was relaxing for us. I'll keep my eyes open for a hops farm.

We arrived in Seattle on time, where it was colder than we expected for late October. Nina's cousin Art, who lives in Seattle, met us at the station. He wanted to show us around the city. We had to make it very clear to him that this was a working vacation because we were tasting beers. He laughed, but understood.

Seattle is located on Puget Sound and is nestled between the Olympic Mountains to the West and the Cascades to the East. Mt. Rainier stands tall to the Southeast and is clearly visible from the downtown area. Its history starts with logging and fishing in the early 1800's. The local historians are proud of their almost comedic roots and quirky personalities.

Our first stop was Pike Brewing Company, which is most centrally located at Pike Place Market. Charles Finkel founded it in the mid 80's being one of the first in the craft beer revolution. Charles is also the founder of Merchant du Vin, an importer of specialty beers from Belgium and Germany. It's a roomy brew pub with a medium sized bar. The menu has just been revamped to fit the times and location. My first beer was a Tandem Double Ale, which tasted as if it had a little bit of wheat used in the brewing process, smooth and delicious. It went well with my salmon sandwich. Nina was surprised to find that the guest beer on tap for the week was Ayinger Celebrator Bock from Germany. This is one of her all time favorites. She departed from the plan of drinking local brews to savor her favorite. It's forgivable. She followed that up with a Tandem Double ale and enjoyed it also. My second beer was the Kilt Lifter, a brown ale smooth and delicious.

Our second stop was Bistro 1200, up in the Capital Hill area East of the waterfront and Interstate 5, which slices through the city. I was a little surprised at Art's selection of places because it was not a brewpub or a beer bar. But to my surprise they had some interesting beers on tap. I suppose you don't have to worry about that here in the Northwest. Choose a nice restaurant to dine in and most likely, there will be a fine selection of beers to choose from.

I selected a Hefeweizen from Maritime Pacific Brewing, located in Seattle. It was smooth, and the clove spiciness was not overpowering. My second choice was Manny's Pale ale from Georgetown Brewing, also from Seattle. This beer may have been the best that I have had on this journey. Clean, pleasant, refreshing, I wanted another. For some reason Nina started to drink martinis. No more beer for her today. No more cell phone either. Oops, she left it at the bar! Neither of us notices until the morning.

We are very lucky on this trip to the Northwest because the weather has really been good. My vision of the area is a lot of rain, especially in the winter months. But we haven't seen a drop of rain since we arrived. Today is another blue-sky sunny day. We walk to the Northern end of town to see the famous Space Needle. From the top we could see Baker Mountain in the East which is 160 miles away. Mt. Rainier in the South was poking its peak above the clouds on the horizon.

After leaving the Space Needle, we walked back to Bistro 1200 to retrieve the phone. It wasn't out of our way because a few blocks away was Elysian Brewing Company on East Pike Street. Upon entering, I notice banners on the wall celebrating their winnings at the GABF, Great American Beer Festival. Elysian has won Large Brew Pub of the year in 1999, 2003, and 2004. Recently they received the gold medal award for their Dragonstooth Stout.

I was happy to see that they also brew a lager and a pilsner. I gave the Zephyrus Pils a taste and was pleased with the balance; it was a good example of a pilsner. Along with a lunch, Nina and I proceeded to taste the ESB, Bette Blanche, Achilles Amber, IPA, Dragonstooth stout, and Dortmund. That's a long list, I guess we like these beers. The ESB was nice and rounded, full of flavor yet not heavy on the hops. The Bette Blanche was a Belgian Triple, sweet, good color, nice foam lace on the glass, and hints of coriander. The Achilles Amber even though a respectable 5.9%, was a great session beer, but we can't stick to just one flavor. Dragonstooth stout was black and delicious, just smooth going down. The Dortmund was heavy on the hops.

We start a conversation with Dave Buhler one of the founders of Elysian. We tell him we're on a bit of a pub crawl and that we love his beers. He pours us a taste of the IPA, which is smooth and just the right amount of hops in it for us. He tells us that Elysian has just opened another unit across from the Quest Field on the waterfront. The larger space offers more dining options with the same beers. Sounds great to us, I hope we can make it. These beers are just right on the money as far as taste goes.

Speaking with Dave we get on the subject of travels for beer and Antwerp, Belgium. He too has been to the beer bar named Kulminator. Nina and I had just visited there six months ago. The Kulminator is well known in the beer world as maybe the greatest place to find a beer. Remember, they offer Chimay by the year, and their beer menu is as thick as the Bible! It's funny that people from around the world focus and gather at one place to meet and satisfy their beer desires. We felt connected to Dave, but it was time to move on.

We had a good 45-minute walk back downhill to the waterfront. I say "downhill" because Seattle consists of seven hills, and the waterfront is the low point of the city. On our way, of course we find another pub, McMenamins Six Arms. This is a unique pub, which seemed to be designed and built from scrap pieces. Basic plumbing pipe is used throughout for rails and barriers. Having it decorated for Halloween really made it feel strange. We didn't like the beers here, so we didn't stay long.

We arrive back at Pike Place Market just about sunset. It is a nice place to see the sunset over Puget Sound. Nina and I look for a place to have a beer and enjoy the scenery. We find a restaurant called Place Pigalle. Not to worry about the beer selection, they have a good selection on tap. I select from Hales Ales the special bitter. The taste of the beer reminds me of the London beers. A good session bitter, amber color, and a thick white head. Nina has the Naughty Nellie from Pike Brewing. It had an amber color, smooth, with mild spiciness.

The sun goes down, and we are out the door. Our next stop is the Virginia Inn. Not a brewpub, but an interesting bar with local art covering the walls. Here is an interesting group of people. There are about a dozen and half beers on tap from the area.

Our last stop of the day was the Central Saloon. Just a few blocks South of the Market, it is Seattle's oldest bar, established in 1892, just after one of Seattle's major fires. We feel a little out of place here. The bar is stocked with a great selection of beers and a very stylistic antique bar back. The music is loud, progressive, and the crowd is a little rough for us. I would love to stay and do some sampling but, one beer and we're out.

The next day is Halloween and Nina's birthday. Happy Birthday Nina! We do some sightseeing at the Underground and the Aquarium. It's a slow pace day. We decide to have dinner at the Fairmont Hotel and try different samplings from the menu. Again our bartender is friendly and knowledgeable about the beers that are on tap. He has a good collection of brews from the area.

Nina and I sample different beers with local seafood appetizers and dinner. Great combinations and they are all very fulfilling.

The next morning is our travel day and we have to say good-bye to the Northwest. The people and the beers really did live up to their hype. I found one postcard/beer mat that I purchased and brought home with me. It shows a mug of beer as a cartoon character with a proud smile on it saying "Greetings from THE BIG BEERS of the GREAT NORTHWEST. Recognized as the cradle of the craft beer revival, come the biggest, boldest beers in the world". I won't argue with that. Big and bold they were!

Kudos to the people of the area, who know what they have, and are lucky to enjoy it everyday.

When we arrived home, we met a brewer friend of ours, Fran, who brews the beers for Brewzzi in Florida. We told him about our trip to the Northwest and he just rolled his eyes in envy. He knows we have tasted some great beers. He asked us our favorite and we told him the beers from Elysian. Fran recognized the brand and the brewer Dick Cantwell, who is known as a guru of the business. Well, I'm glad then that we had the best, but they were all the best.

Thanks Portland and Seattle. I think we'll be back for one of your outdoor beer festivals next year.

LONDON AND BATH, ENGLAND

Next stop England. Most people, even if you have not been there, have heard of the famous British Pubs. Any beer drinker who notices the beers available at their local bar at home knows that England has some good beers to offer. So the next travels for beer is two nights in Bath and five nights in London.

The people of England drink more ale than any other country. Ales vary in color from a pale gold to a dark ruby red or brown copper. The strength of these beers varies from about 3.5 to 4.5% alcohol by volume. These beers are brewed for drinking in quantity, and in company. The principal type of ale served is a bitter.

At home in the US we are familiar with the names Bass, New Castle, Fullers and Boddington. These can be found quite easily in a good pub. Bass is available in bottles and draft, New Castle usually by bottle, Fullers London Pride, ESB, and Porter are available at an English Pub in the US in both bottles and draft. Boddington can be found in those nitrogen packed cans, which are very tasty and creamy.

If you do any research before going to England, you will probably find out about an organization named CAMRA. The Campaign for Real Ale. Visit their website camra.org.uk, and you will find plenty of information including pub guides and beer events. CAMRA is an independent, voluntary, consumer organization, which campaigns for real ale, real pubs and consumer rights. What is real ale? It can be also known as "cask conditioned" beer, where the yeast is still present in the container from which the beer is served. Because the beer is not pasteurized, the yeast is still alive, and the process of fermentation continues in the cask, or keg, or bottle, on the way to the consumer. This gives it a fresh and natural taste.

CAMRA is against the mass produced pasteurized beers and in favor of preserving and the serving of real ale. Those are great intentions. But, cask ale needs much attention by knowledgeable pub owners and bartenders. When the cask arrives at the pub, it needs to undergo its second fermentation before being served. Real ale is served at a cool temperature of between 54 and 57 degrees. It is cooler than room temperature but warmer than the refrigerator. This correct temperature enhances the flavors of the ale.

The cellar person of the pub must tend to these casks and monitor the process of the second fermentation. He or she decides when the beer is ready to be served. This beer will not remain fresh forever. It has a very limited life span, usually dependent upon its alcohol level. No gas is used to force the beer from the cask up to the bar and out a spigot. Instead, a "beer engine" is used at the bar top and the bartender actually pulls or siphons the beer from the cask. The result should be a real ale served at the proper temperature, less carbonated, and highly tasty.

I'm glad CAMRA exists to promote quality, choice, and value at the local public house. However, I worry that the less skilled bartender may not be up to the task of protecting our beloved beer. A second independent body called Cask Marque Trust is a non-profit organization and it initiated a program where member pubs are visited unannounced by an assessor. The assessor will check all cask ales on sale for temperature, appearance, aroma and taste. If the pub passes, it receives a framed certificate and merchandising material to inform its customers of their achievement. You can visit their website at www.caskmarque.co.uk

Why was the Cask Marque Program initiated? Cask ale sales had declined in the 90's and were gaining a bad reputation. A survey was conducted using qualified auditors who visited over 1,000 pubs throughout England of which 82% served traditional cask ale. Their findings showed that 23% of the pubs were serving beer that the auditors would not buy again. The major reasons were too many different beer pulls at the bar and a failure to serve the beer at the proper temperature. The program has had some success. Now owners are aware of their problems and are spending money on new delivery systems and better cooling systems.

When you receive cask ale that is warmer than recommended, or old beyond its recommended days it is not a pleasant experience. Cask ale is the champagne of the beer world. It needs ever-loving care. I compare it to experiencing warm red wine in a restaurant. There is nothing more disappointing than paying $15 for a glass of red that arrives at room temperature and not cellar temperature. Too few restaurants chill their wines served by the glass. I am tired of drinking those hot red wines, and now I am forcing myself to simply refuse them. "Mind the blimey sour pint of ale, please!"

While doing your research before going to England, you will find plenty of pub-crawls pre-designed for you. All you need to do is Google London pub-crawls and many suggestions will come up.

While in London we found out about a crawl called the Monopoly Pub Crawl, monopolypubcrawl.org.uk. They have a suggested route of 26 different pubs! A tall order in deed. It seems you earn a "hotel" for visiting each of the 26 pubs and having alcohol in each. You can earn a "house" for visiting all the pubs but not having a drink in each. Seems like fun. The site tour lists tube and bus routes to reach the pubs.

Another fun crawl idea that I read about is using the Circle Line of the underground subway system. The Circle Line completes a loop through the main core of the city, including nearly two-dozen stops. The idea is to purchase your one-day ticket, ride the Circle Line and get off at each stop along the route. Once you are on street level stop in at the closest pub and have a pint!

Simpler and less exhausting ideas are to just select an area of the city and focus on those pubs within that area. Go for a nice walk along either side of the Thames River and visit some of the historical pubs there. Or, concentrate your efforts in the Holborn area where the pubs of justice and law are situated. On the South side of the Thames near London Bridge are some great pubs in the Borough area.

At a good bookstore or on the web you can purchase books specifically on London Pubs or English Pubs. I own a few of these books, and after reading and choosing the one's I would like to visit, I plot them on a tourist map. This map, along with some tourist highlights becomes very handy.

For instance, after you have spent an hour or two watching the changing of the guard at Buckingham Palace you will be ready for a pint, and your handy map will point you to the closest pub. Or, maybe you just walked 30 minutes along the Thames River to see the Tower Bridge and worked up a thirst. Pull out your handy map and find your favorite pub marked for the area. Then after you've had some fish 'n chips and a couple of pints, head into the Tower of London and see the torture chambers or Royal Jewels.

Don't pick just any pub. In London there are thousands of pubs, they seem to be everywhere. Use your own guide and use your eyes to be selective. There are good pubs and bad pubs. I don't like the modern looking ones. I'm here in London for tradition, not a revolution. On previous visits, I had learned that the beer can be risky as far as quality goes. If you find that pub with the warm cellar, your beer may be flat, sour, and not pleasing. We found this to be true more times than we expected. We never returned a pint, but wanted to. Nina had no problem with ordering half pints.

A good cask ale is smooth, very flavorful, not overly carbonated, and goes down quick and easy. The alcohol levels are a little lower, around 3.5 to 5%, making for a great session beer. Session, meaning you can spend some time at a pub and converse with friends for long periods without getting drunk. That is the purpose of the pub isn't it? Traditionally, your session was used to gather news of the day, talk with neighbors and conduct business or eat a meal.

The pubs of England were the center of everyday life. The pubs were designed to fit the lifestyle of the people around it. Some pubs were located in the areas where the business of justice was practiced and the pubs were visited by the lawyers. Other pubs were located in the shipping area. The food, the beer, the design, the whole pub was designed for the life that went on around it.

Now today in the modern world we can visit all of them! My last visit in 2004 was with three other lads including my restaurant manager, Matt. We stuck with a plan and probably visited 40 pubs in three days. A good, consistent pace. We definitely had at least one pint in each. Some pints were not finished though due to quality.

There are no beer styles or flavors to wow you here. You will see beers labeled bitter, best, and ale, which all seem close in flavor. Other selections include an occasional IPA with a very slight hop kick, or an ESB, or some very good stouts. In my opinion, the golden beers are not very tasty. For comparison, in Germany you could choose from a crisp hoppy pilsner, a malty sweet Oktoberfest beer, a tart weisse, or a deep rich bock. Distinct differences in flavors and mouth feel, and each very delicious. Therefore, I've decided that this trip's pub-crawl will primarily be for architectural ideas. A pub-crawl for tasting the flavors of the pubs themselves!

These historic pubs of England are just beautiful and are unmatched. Mostly designed and built with dark woods, they are very dressed up with colorful tiles, etched glass, stained glass, embossed ceilings and walls, elegant light fixtures, and plenty of mirrors. So Nina and I will hoist enough pints, but we'll also be hoisting the camera to take lots of photos. We're looking for ideas to use in a pub we may open some day soon.

Some of these pubs are tiny in size. It's not uncommon for the pub to be only 20' x 20' but jammed with character. When you open the door, you'll be greeted with the strong smell of cigarettes and smoke. Sometimes it made us choke. Soon this will end though, with a proposed smoking ban to begin in July of 2007. I hope it works and saves the pubs. It seems everyone smokes here, so maybe it will not be successful. I'm familiar with both Florida and New Jersey where no smoking prevails, and it became law with ease, despite initial complaints. But those were states where only about 25% of the people smoked, so it will be interesting to see what happens in England.

When you enter the pub, grab your own table and don't wait for service. You'll be waiting a long time for a beer or food. Everything is ordered through the bartender and paid for, when ordered. The beers are clearly marked on the beer engine and probably on a chalkboard also.

The pub rooms may be small, but they pack many seats into the small space. Small tables, small chairs and stools. There are many ledges on the walls to hold your pint glass. The corners may have a snug. A snug is a small booth with short walls surrounding the benches and table. An area quite "snugable".

The larger pubs are sometimes divided into smaller rooms. Each room may have its own small fireplace or stove. The pub owner uses these often with the cool, usually damp weather.

TV's don't exist in the pubs. It reminds you that you are here to make conversation. Music is rarely heard inside a pub. Mostly you hear just the sound of conversation. Newspapers are normally found on the bartop.

The publicans, or pub owners, and the bartenders are always friendly. Give a glance to the people sitting next to you and you are going to get a hello followed by some conversation.

I'm always intriqued by the number of signs used in the pub to tell the customers where the toilets are. There seem to be six or eight loudly pointing you in the direction. The direction is most likely in the rear of the pub and downstairs. So why so many signs? I also noticed that the "Gents" is usually very close to the bar, while the "Ladies" is never nearby.

It's a long journey to England from Florida where we started. It took us 21 hours from the start of our travels to Bath, traveling 4000 miles. We landed at Gatwick Airport, which is 30 miles South of London. From Gatwick we traveled two and a half hours by train to Bath in the West.

Bath is approximately 30 miles from the Western Coast. The River Avon runs through the center. The river has the Pulteney Bridge crossing it which will remind anyone who has been to Florence, Italy, of the Ponte de Vechio bridge in a smaller version. The town is named after a natural spring, which delivers one million liters of water per day at 120 degrees. The Romans found this spring 2000 years ago and built a temple and baths around the spring. These baths and Temple are necessary to see, restored to their original grandeur. Bath in the eighteenth century was the place to be for the rich and famous. The local architecture is Georgian and striking, using a honey colored stone which gives you a mellow feeling.

The prominent Bath Abbey is the largest gothic church in England. It is over 500 years old and located on a site that has had a house of worship for more than 1000 years. This church is still very active.

The streets of the city are narrow and always turning, making pub hunting a lot of fun in the small alleys. A guide will help you find the historic ones, but wander around and you will find something.

I selected a hotel from the Internet, and saw that the hotel's bar featured Abbey Ales, which are brewed locally in Bath. Seemed like a good hotel to me! We found ourselves at their bar minutes after checking in. Their website fooled me a bit because although they featured Abbey Ales they served only one at any one time. So, our first beer was the Abbey Ales' Bellringer. The Bellringer is 4.2%, light bodied, but a nice dry bitter finish, amber gold in color.

Abbey Ales is the first new brewery in this historic city in forty years and has only been brewing for ten years. Situated within site of the Bath Abbey, the beers are only delivered to pubs within a twenty-mile radius. The brewery produces beers with some clever names; Christer, Resurrection, Steeplejack, Salvation, Twelfth Night, White Friar and Black Friar. We'll keep an eye out for these varieties.

I had brought with me a list of pubs to visit, but I also quickly found two publications in the hotel lobby describing pubs to visit and a little history of each pub. I love it when the town assists you in your pub-crawl; it's just so friendly of them. It's drizzling rain outside today as we start our hunt. Luckily, the hotel is situated just on the edge of the town center, so it is not far to anywhere.

We wander into the Old Green Tree pub on Green Street of course. A historic pub on the list to visit, it is the third oldest license in Bath, built in the early 18th Century. It's good to get out of the rain, but inside we are greeted by smoke, lots of smoke. The pub has three little rooms including the bar room and one non-smoking room in the rear. The bar has seats for four, and the rear room has about five tables. Each room measures no more than 10 x 10. We're greeted with a friendly hello and move to the rear room. We are hungry, but select our pints before ordering food. They offer Abbey Ale Twelfth Night and Mr. Pereets stout, both very tasty and delivered in good shape. The Twelfth Night is a winter warmer, ruby in color, and full of malt flavors. The menu was limited and we shared a bowl of soup with bread.

Just to get out of the rain, our next stop was a youth hostel named Christophers. Nina and I both enjoyed a Bombardier premium bitter here. Bombardier is 4.3%, copper in color and branded as "The drink of England". It is brewed using the brewery's own well water and fermented for seven days. They were fresh and pleasing.

Our last stop was at a modern bar named Revolution (and I thought I wasn't looking for a revolution in a bar). They had some interesting marketing ideas here. A well rounded beer list along with lots of vodka. There were two flat screen TV's behind the bar which constantly blitzed you with commercials for the place, their drinks, and a self improvement guide which they sold. The self-improvement guide included information on how to better drink more vodka. They sell shots of vodka in dozens of flavors, in large groupings. They had Staropromen pilsner from the Czech Republic on draft, so I couldn't pass that up. It was cold and delicious.

In the morning, we purchased our tickets for the hop on, hop off, bus tour around the city. It was a small city, but these tours are usually worth the money to see the major sites quickly.

At lunchtime, we find ourselves at Bath's Pub of the Year for 2006, The Raven. Another small sized pub with two levels. The first floor is very enchanting, and the upper level is smoke free for groups. The bar seats about six, with six tables placed around the outer walls of the room. The tables are small but everyone seems to find a place for their lunch and pint. There is lots of wood here. The beer selection is good with a half dozen selections of cask ale. The owners are building a reputation of serving great food. They offer a good selection of English pies. An English pie is a combination of fillings in a pie like crust, typically served with chips (fries) and gravy. My pie was stuffed with parsnip, roasted chestnuts, rosemary, onion and cheddar cheese with a Guinness and red wine gravy. Delicious, I could have eaten two.

It's late afternoon, and chilly. The rain has stopped for now. We find a little pub, not on our list or map. Little is the right way to describe it. We are already use to small, but walking into this pub, it is real small. Not more than 10 x 16 feet. In fact, it is the smallest in Bath. Tiny Coeur-de-Lion is a pretty pub both inside and out. The outside is painted blue, with a large window made of many small panes across the front, and a colorful wooden sign. I must say that the pubs in England all have some great, colorful, whimsical sign mounted outside to announce the name of their pub.

The bar seats four, with five tables set up around the room. The wall with the windows has a banquette to be used with two of the tables. There is a sign above the bench that reads "Get friendly and please BUDGE UP". I guess that means to squish your butts together to squeeze more people in.

It was like sitting in someone's living room. We met a local, Joe, with an unpleasant disposition, who eventually bought us a round of beers. We tried to say no several times, but hey, the dollar is in bad shape here against the

British Pound, and we could use the help. Thanks Joe! We also spoke with another gent who was an arm chair travel writer. He recommended a walk to the Star Tavern. It's on our list, so we make a point of getting there on our last night in Bath.

After two beers at the Lion and two lungs full of smoke, we moved onto a modern stop, All Bar One. We were hungry and they had a fun tapas menu. The food was all good. They had a great beer selection also, including some bottles. So I needed to rinse out my inners and enjoyed a refreshing Schneider Weiss from Germany. It really hit the spot. I followed that up with a bottle of Leffe from Belgium and Staropramen from Czech. Nina broke even more rules and sipped some champagne.

The Star Inn was worth the hike. On the opposite side of town, it was drizzling again, but we walked it in quick time. The pub was first licensed in 1759 and was built in the shape of a coffin by its owner who had a sense of humor. There are no game machines, no music, no tv, and no air circulation. But the place is beautiful. There are four small rooms, and three of them had their own fireplace or stove. Tiny rooms here.

When we arrived, the crowd seemed to follow us. Trying to get our first round of beers was tough, having to wait on a queue. It seems the bartender got a little stressed when some people ordered cocktails and a glass of wine. Where are the mixers? Where is the corkscrew? Why can't they just drink beer? Finally, when he gets back to doing the natural thing of pulling a beer, he states loudly, "The beers taste better when you have to wait for them!"

He was right. They serve quality beer here. I enjoyed an Adnams Bitter and Nina got to try another Abbey Ale, the Twelfth Night, the winter seasonal. Adnams has been brewing beers since 1872 using only English hops and malts. The Bitter is 3.7%, dry but refreshing. It is a top ten seller of cask ale in England.

We met two locals at our shared table. A young man had just picked up his father in law for the purpose of seeing his new grandchild. Their stop at the pub was also planned. We shared jokes, noting that America and England were two great countries separated by a common language. We also talked about beer and of course George Bush. Everyone seems to want to talk about politics. I try to change the subject as quickly as possible. We had fun with our new friends, they even bought us a round! Our second round of free beers since we arrived in Bath. They extended their pickup time by their wives so they could enjoy another beer with us. They were drinking Bass, the first time I had seen it on tap in England.

Our local friends pointed us in the direction of another well-visited pub, The Bell. The Bath branch of CAMRA voted The Bell as its 2004 Pub of the Year. When we arrived and opened the door, all heads turned to see who it was. Not a good sign, but as long as you drink beer, you are okay. Doesn't seem too historical, but it has been important to the area for bringing live jazz music to its visitors. They offer at least half dozen cask ales, sticking to the local brews. Seemed like a young crowd, a couple of large rooms and an outside sitting area.

We leave Bath in the morning with a good feeling inside. The people were friendly, even our grumpy friend Joe. The crowds were younger than we expected but that is explained by the presence of Bath University. The food we ate was good. I would estimate that 15% of our draft beers were barely drinkable. This is not a good way to start five days of pubs in London.

A train gets us to London's Paddington Station around lunchtime on a Friday. Mass transportation in London is quick and easy to navigate. Five major train stations are located around the city in geographical areas. Each station handles trains arriving and departing to an appropriate area of the compass for England or Europe. Paddington is in the Northwest corner of London and handles train traffic to the West of London including the city of Bath. When coming to and from London via train be aware of which station you are arriving at, or departing from. You could miss your connections.

The famous London Tube, or subway system, is easy to figure out, and is clean and quick. Our hotel was located across the city in actual old City of London, and we opted for an official London Taxi Cab ride. Take the cab once, and notice the available space within the backseat. Just take your bags with you to your seat! Chat with the cabbie, they are usually very friendly, and you can get yourself accustomed to the accent and the language.

Our hotel was located just outside the boundary of the actual City of London on the North side of the Thames River near Black Friars Bridge. The City of London is really only one square mile, which includes most of the old sections. Mostly the financial district now, but it does include the wonderful church of St. Paul. If you stay in this area, be aware that on weekends, it is a ghost town and the pubs will be closed. Our location seems central to the major tourist sites, the River, and some good pub-crawl areas.

After checking in at the hotel, we hurry out on to the streets to find a place for lunch. We go in the direction of the Thames and quickly find the Wellington on Strand Street. Not on our list of pubs to visit, but looks good and is crowded. We luck out with a table on the second level. Traditionally decorated, but I doubt if it is historic. I figure I might as well have my first order of Fish N Chips. When it arrives, I'm surprised at the size of the fish. Must have been a cousin of Moby Dick. Try the Fish N Chips at least once, it's usually good, but watch for a good price. I've seen the price vary from 7-16 British Pounds without much difference in appearance. The beer here was also delicious and obviously well cared for.

When we finish lunch it is after 2pm and because of the early setting sun in winter, it will be dark by 4pm. Since it is Nina's first visit, we decide to take in the major sites with a walk along the Thames River. We walked along the river towards Big Ben and the Parliament Buildings. Along the way you can see the Tate Museum, Justice Hall, and a few WWII monuments.

Soon we approach Big Ben. We all know Big Ben. Ben is really the name of the clock and not the tower that it sits atop. It's 150 years old and is on the end of the Westminster Palace or Parliamentary Buildings. From Big Ben it is a quick walk to Westminster Abbey and St. Margaret's Church.

From there, you can follow the park trails to Buckingham Palace. Outside the gates is a massive statue of Queen Victoria. We overheard a fellow tourist state, "Hay, que faia!" Nina roughly translates this to, "Wow, she is very ugly" in Spanish. The evening lights were just beginning to come on, and the city took on another look.

We walked back along the mall towards Trafalgar Square and the huge statue of Lord Nelson overlooking the busy intersection. Without looking at our map we head towards the hotel walking down Long Acre Street. There are many theatres and pubs in this area. Very lively, it has a good feel about it. Jackpot. We're thirsty and in the right area.

Our first pub sign that we see is on the sidewalk pointing around the corner to a pub named Walkers of Whitehall. The sign reads "It's bigger than you think!" Okay, we'll check it out. Cute place. There are plenty of business people ending their hectic week. I had a cold London Pride from Fullers and Nina had a Fullers ESB. We enjoyed them. The place had a large downstairs area with just a small main bar on the street level.

Fullers has been brewing in London for more than 150 years. The London Pride bitter is 4.1%, session strength, with a malt base and well defined hop flavors. The ESB is 5.5% from the cask and is rich, malty, with tangy fruit flavors, and spicy hops. The ESB has won many awards during the years including CAMRA's Best Strong Ale for 1978, 79, 81, 83, 85, 87, and 1991.

The area is very busy with Friday revelers and theatergoers. We stumble upon Salisbury, a pub on the list to visit. Known for its ornate décor, it lives up to its reputation. Filled with people and smoke, we luck out with two spots to lean at the bar. We wanted to try Old Hooky, but the cellar man was just tapping it up and it wasn't ready. I quickly realized that we need to come back again to really get a good look at this place when it is less busy. Two quick pints and we're gone (okay, one pint and one half pint).

We continue in the direction of the hotel, walking through the Covent Garden Area, and pass numerous pubs. All busy. All smoky. We had a couple of good pints and a couple of bad pints. The highlight of the trek back were a group of outdoor lights that we came upon. They were actually outdoor chandeliers hanging across several intersections. They must have measured about ten feet across and as many feet tall. They were very beautiful with crystal and candles. They were located at several intersections. We don't know what they are from or what their purpose is, but we'll try to find out.

We come across our hotel quicker than expected. Not surprisingly, we are not ready to call it a night yet. So we dump off our day packs and decide to have one more pint. I know by my trusty map that a pub which figures to be a highlight of the tour is just around the corner, I hope.

The Princess Louise promises to be right out of the Victorian era and well preserved.

We found the Princess right where she has been standing since 1872. On the not so ornate exterior, the sign proclaims a Free House. A Free House means the pub is not affiliated with any of the major brewers, and any named beer can be poured there. Louise was the fourth daughter of Queen Victoria. When we walked into the place it was fully occupied, but the fabulous décor just could not be missed. The fantastic glass and mirrors were both beveled and etched. The mosaic tiling found on both the floors and walls are sometimes picturesque. I had to actually go over to the wall and touch it to see if the picture really was made from tiles. The large first floor bar is dark mahogany wood and seats about two dozen. One side of the main room has tables along the wall. It's not large, probably 30 x 40.

After drinking one pint, Nina and I walk upstairs to see what is there. Another large room grandly decorated. The staff was cleaning up for the night and we mentioned to them how beautiful the room looked. One girl responded that the real beauty is downstairs, upstairs was "too cosmetic". We took that to mean that it was not original and that it was recently added to the pub.

The next morning we hop on the tour bus for a city tour. As I have mentioned before, these are usually great buys and give you a feel and layout for the city. London is big, so it is advantageous to see it from the bus. We get lucky with our Saturday purchase, because our ticket is good for 48 hours instead of the usual 24. We start the tour at Aldwych Street and the bus drives East. We pass St. Paul's Cathedral, the Bank of England, the Fire Monument, Tower of London, and pass over the Tower Bridge before heading back West. The bus continues along the Thames River until we reach Big Ben and the House of Parliament where it crosses the river and comes back behind Westminster Abbey.

There are many tourist sites in London. You can hop off this bus anywhere, and then hop back on anywhere you please. We then pass through the ritzy area of Belgrave, pass Victoria Station, and further West past Buckingham Palace and St. James Park. We get off the bus on the East end of Hyde Park. We have an idea of trying to purchase tickets to the show, *The Sound of Music*. It is a remake of course, but we are close, somewhere, to the theater. Maybe we can get lucky for a Saturday night ticket!

We find the theater, but only after hopping off the bus and realizing that, we still have a distance to walk ahead of us. We need to walk to the Soho area. It was matinee time and people were lining up to get unused "will call" tickets. No chance of that! Let's go to the box office and see what's available. A very friendly gent working the window hooks us up with tickets for Monday night's performance. Awesome! Time to celebrate. Where is the closest pub? No need for a map, we just walk out of the theater and there is the Argyll Arms. I think it's on our list.

The Argyll Arms looks good from the outside, with its black and gold nameplate, and people sitting outside even on this chilly, drizzly day. But walking into the Argyll is another story. Long and narrow, with tall ceilings, it displays another brilliant interior highly decorated. The first floor is divided into smaller, little snugs, with glass or wood. Each passage way is complete with a wooden arch. You can never forget to look up in a place like this either. The ceiling is either embossed tin or molded plaster with ornate details. The front small snugs open up to a larger room in the rear. This larger room has a large brass and crystal chandelier hanging. Towards the rear is a very nice, sweeping, wooden staircase to the upstairs, with a larger room.

The main bar has a sign stating, "no smoking at the bar". Thank goodness for that, but it really doesn't help the smoke problem. We enjoy a half pint of Guinness and a pint of Abbott ale. Both cool and fresh. Greene King brews the Abbott ale, which is 5%, with a ripe fruit character, malty richness, and superb hop balance and goes down smooth. This is a place where you could spend the day. Looking around, I think some people are with their newspapers and books in front of them. It is a busy Saturday afternoon in a busy area of London, a perfect place.

We decide to wander a couple of blocks in either direction to see what we can find as far as pubs go. On Great Portland Street, we find two, The Cock and The George. You can't pass up a huge sign that reads The Cock and not walk in. We do. It's a Sam Smith pub, which is okay because the Sam Smith beers are usually good. We share an Extra Stout and our taste buds prove us right. Sam Smith has been brewing beers since 1758 in Yorkshire, England. The Xtra Stout is 4.5%, dry, and goes down easy. The Cock has an intricate tiled floor, a patterned ceiling, and very nice woodwork including arches and scrolls. Probably new, but nice work.

Across the street was The George and we had two more pints. An Abbott ale for me, and Nina had an Old Speckled Hen. We love the Hen when it is nitrogen pushed at home, like a Guinness pour. This Old Hen was just tired, not too tasty. The Abbott ale, another favorite at home, was not as good as over at the Argyll. The staff was very friendly. The décor was slightly plainer than over at The Cock, but it was very comfortable with upholstered stools and benches, patterned drapes over the windows and etched glass mirrors along the walls. To the side of the main bar area was a small sitting room with dark, wood paneling from floor to ceiling. This room was very welcoming with its warmth.

We know it is time to start our walk home, probably a mile or two. We need to walk down Oxford Street towards Covent Garden and on to the hotel. As we walk, a pub always catches our eyes, and we decide we need another stop. One such stop was the Freemasons Arms, a Shepherd Neame pub. Shepherd Neame is the oldest brewery in Britain started in 1698. It is also the site where in 1863 the Football Association was founded. I selected a bottle of Bishops Fingers, Kentish Strong Ale of 5.4%. This beer was excellent! It was a glass of quenching liquid in this desert of refreshing beer. It seems that this beer is brewed only on Fridays and only uses raw materials from Kent, England. That includes the water, hops, and malt. I think that is pretty cool and strict standards. I also had a Spitfire Bitter. The Spitfire was the WWII English fighter plane used during the Battle of Britain. The beer was developed to raise money for the RAF Benevolent Society. Okay, I'll raise my pint to that, in fact, give me another.

Sunday morning we awake and decide to have service at St. Paul's church. It is only a ten-minute walk from the hotel. The church is about 500 years old and one of the largest in all of Europe. I can't help but remember the history of this church during the Blitz of WWII. Hitler was insistent on bombing England into submission during the Fall and Winter of 1940. Everyday during the nighttime there was constant bombings. Inside the Cathedral, volunteers were strategically situated within the structure of the dome to be on the ready in case any fires started from the bombing. The Cathedral survived the bombings, because of German bad aim or divine intervention. Attending Sunday Mass seemed required for us.

We need lunch. It is time for the trusty pub/tourist map. Well it's Sunday in the East end of town. There is nothing open. I want to visit the Viaduct Tavern, but it is closed. Next is The Old Bell. It is closed. Next is Old

Cheshire Cheese, closed. Further West on Strand Street we find The George, different than yesterday's pub, The George. It was Tudor in style. Why are so many pubs named The George? Because, there have been six Kings by the name of George, the last reigning from 1936 to 1952. He was the father of Elizabeth II, the reigning Queen.

This pub was not on our list, but everything was just great. Carrot soup and spaghetti Bolognese were tasty and plentiful. The beers that we drank, Guinness and Greene King IPA, were just right. Great stop, great pub, friendly staff.

With purchasing the bus tour, our ticket also entitled us to a river cruise. Today is our day, partly sunny, which in London is probably labeled mostly sunny. We want to take advantage of this. We need to walk down to the Tower Bridge and pick up the Cruise ship and then cruise West to Big Ben. Probably just a twenty minute ride, but should be spectacular.

The cruise on the Thames was windy and cold, but full of sights. I could only imagine back in 1620 when the Mayflower set sail for America from this very River. The travelers gathered at a pub then named the Ship located on this River. The pub is still there, now named the Mayflower. Or, imagining more recently, the German Luftwaffe constantly bombing this city. Big Ben appears in front of us rather quickly and it is time to debark.

Just one block North of the River and diagonally across from Big Ben is St. Stephen's Tavern. From the outside, it is brightly lit and very inviting. We want to walk in. From the front door, you enter about three steps above the main bar room and get a very special view. It is like walking into someone's old-tyme parlor. The main room is tall and small in area, but again Victorian in style. Red and gold brightly patterned drapes reach from the ceiling to the floor and the wall color is beige. The main room has small couches and tables, great woodwork, and brightly etched glass and light fixtures. There is something about the colors of dark wood, scarlet and gold that seems so Victorian and so pleasing. The bar back was nearly 16 feet tall and the bar top had four foot lamppost-like, brass light fixtures mounted on it.

Nina and I pull up two stools to a small table next to a window, which faces Big Ben. The window had a Victorian design etched on it. The sun has gone down and the sky has a deep blue tint to it. Through the window, we can see Big Ben, which is just turning on his night-lights, some gold and some green. A photographic moment. Okay, quick, a beer! Badger beers sold here. Tanglefoot for Nina and Festive Pheasant for me.

Hall and Woodhouse, family brewers since 1777, in Dorset, brew Badger beers. The Tanglefoot is a premium ale, full body, medium bitterness, smooth hoppiness and hints of melon and pear. It seems, the name for the beer comes from the night when the head brewer did some sampling of his first batch and had a "sudden loss of steering". The Tanglefoot was served fresh here along with the seasonal ale, Festive Pheasant. A cask ale that is "full-feather flavored". And don't forget their slogan, "a pint of pheasant is exceedingly pleasant"!

We really like it here. This is such a busy tourist area with Big Ben right outside. Yet, inside leaning at the bartop were two local blokes jibber jabbing. I place them as cabbies or limo drivers. While they were talking, they always looked up at Big Ben through the window and were obviously checking the time. They never looked at their watches, if they had watches. I imagined that they both needed to be somewhere at 5 pm because it was now 4:55. I loved the fact that they were using Ben as a time piece and not a photographic subject as were thousands of other people outside. Nina and I were always ducking outside to get yet another picture. These two blokes sipped their beers, told some stories, glanced at Ben and then they were on their way as Ben chimed five deep notes. So were we.

We walked to Trafalgar Square to see it at night. It was worth the short walk. With the fountains and the National Gallery in the background, it reminds you that this is a big city, even though the pubs are small. We know our way home from here. We will pass by the Salisbury again. Good, we need to.

There has been a pub at this location probably since the mid 1800's but it was not called the Salisbury until about fifty years ago. The sign outside has two dates, 1830 and 1903, but I am not sure of the significance. It was beautifully rebuilt in the 1890's using the Victorian style of wood, glass, mirror, and marble. Along one wall are small booths that are separated by small bronze statues of nymphs or Greek goddesses, which have flowery lamps, arching from them. Candles further separate the booths. The fabrics are plush and red in color. The walls are filled with large etched glass panels. Even the brass coat hooks mounted on the pillars are oversize. The main bar is large and made of mahogany. There is a side entrance from St. Marten's Court, which leads into a smaller room with its own tiny bar. There is a silver gilded staircase leading upstairs but a sign indicates it is for management's use only. This is a treasure chest of architecture!

We sample two pints here, the Deuchars IPA and Peeterman's Artois. Deuchars is brewed by Caledonian, located in Edinburgh, Scotland. An IPA of 4.4% it is cask conditioned. Caledonian is the last of the Edinburgh breweries. Deuchars has a full malt flavor, zesty hopiness, and it was poured well here. I want to take many photos here, but don't want to use the flash and ruin everyone's night. I try my best to take photos without the flash and hope for the best.

Monday morning it is raining and the coldest yet for this trip. We hope to be allowed entrance on the tour bus because our 48 hours ends in an hour. As long as we are on board, we can stay on and finish our tour. We hop on along the River and continue the trip to the West beyond Kensington Palace, Knightsbridge, Royal Albert Hall, and the Royal Music University. We hop off in the Soho area and hope to do some antique looking and pub hunting. It is suppose to be the antique area, but we don't seem to find any. However, we do find some pubs.

One of our first stops is the Running Footman. Not such a dressy pub in architecture and design, but a historic marker on the wall told a good story. During the times of horse carriages and torchlights, a wealthy carriage owner would employ a footman to run alongside his carriage with a lamp. The purpose of the lamp was to see and measure space between passing carriages. The footman also was used to pay any taxes along the route. Or, maybe his job was to order a pint and a sandwich before the master arrived at the pub.

A couple of twisted blocks away is the Red Lion. This pub was located at a point on a tree-lined road where it veered to the right. When you open the door you feel at ease. The well-worn wooden floor creaks when you walk across it. The main bar is in the center and topped with stained glass inserts. Small tables and stools surround the bar. A food menu is mounted on the wall listing potato jackets, which are stuffed potatoes. They can come with cheddar cheese, beans and cheese or salmon and hollandaise sauce. There is a room off to the side with a fireplace. The pub was built in 1752, the old pane windows remain. The walls are decorated simply, and on this cold day, it feels very warm.

We then wandered down the streets, took a couple of turns without the map, and stumbled upon our next pub, the Shepherds Tavern. Built in the 1730's, this pub is located on a square that is surrounded by today's rich. The exterior is painted a bright red. The pub has a medium size mahogany bar and a large bay window enhances the seating area. During WWII, the tavern became a home away from home to the RAF pilots. They could gather here and actually see a chalk scoreboard with the Luftwaffe kills for the week.

It is now time for a quick something to eat and off to the hills of Austria for *The Sound of Music*, coincidently set during WWII.

On our last day in London, we visited the Winston Churchill Museum and War Rooms. This is very cool if you have an interest in WWII. The War Rooms are the actual underground rooms that the government operated from during the war. They remain unchanged since last occupied. Adjacent to the War Rooms is the Churchill Museum, which vividly depicts his life. It brings to life the tragedy and the conditions that Londoners had to live through at that time. One quote I found in the Musuem for Mr. Churchill was "I always believed in staying in the pub until closing time". Old Winston didn't have time for the pubs while he was Prime Minister, but I'm sure before and after his war years he did his share of hoisting.

At this point, I need to apologize to my British friends. Nina and I are getting a little tired of the English ales. We need something to excite our tastebuds and decide to search out a Belgian bar. A quick Google search finds us a place just a few blocks from where our hotel is.

We walk in the door of Belgo and are standing along a glass wall over-looking the kitchen of the restaurant. The smells are appetizing and the warmth from the grills and ovens are welcoming.

The staff members are dressed in monks' outfits. How perfect is that? Our first glance at the menu tells us we picked the right place. They had five of the seven Trappist ales and numerous other Belgian brews along with some Belgian food. We laugh and claim to stay here for both lunch and dinner. We order bottles of Westmalle dubbel and Achel brown.

For food, we start with mussels Provencal. Mussels steamed in white wine, celery and leeks, and served with dark bread for "mopping" up the juices. We follow up the mussels with an order of wild boar sausages. The sausages were served with a sauce made with a berry and Chimay reduction. Excellent. We ordered a side of Belgian Mash. We guess that the mash potatoes were flavored with parsnips, carrots and cabbage. They were very scrumptious. This food pairs with the famous beers superbly. We're so happy we call the manager over to the table and compliment him.

He turns around and buys us a round of six shots of different flavored vodkas *#@!^? Thank you. We find out from him, and the menu, that there is a smaller version of Belgo bar around the corner from our hotel named Bierodrome. Okay, let's go. This is the fastest we have moved since we got here.

The Bierodrome, is located on busy Kensington Hall Road and is filling up quickly. It's a modern and sleek bar, roomy with full size tables and chairs. There is a large center bar with all the Belgian stemware neatly hanging from a brass rack. The beer list is about the same as Belgo, maybe a few more selections. We order Triple Karmeliet and Kasteel. It's a great stop.

We get motivated to visit some more pubs. I want to stop at some classics. We begin a walk down High Holborn towards the Viaduct Tavern. Since 1869, this pub has been standing on a site where public hangings were once held. However, nothing inside will remind you of that. This ornate pub has large, painted mirrors on the walls depicting some artistic statues. It has an intricate ceiling and many etched glass screens. The mahogany bar is round and seems filled with business people. To this day, much of the interior is still original. A sign within notes a permanent ghostly resident in the cellar, affectionately known as Fred.

By this time, Nina and I were ready for a good dinner. We hoped to get a table at Ye Olde Cheshire Cheese, one of the oldest pubs in London located on Fleet Street. In 1666, there was a huge fire and most everything burned in London City. A 202-foot tall tower was built to commemorate the fire. The tower stands 202 feet from where the fire started. The Cheshire Cheese was built just a year later.

The main sign for the pub is on Fleet Street, but the main entrance is down a narrow side alley. You will notice along the side of the door, mounted outside, is a plaque listing in chronological order the British Monarchs. It's worth a notice because some of them have probably stopped here. The royal names end with Queen Elizabeth II. Who is next? Opening the door lets you into 17th and 18th Century London, when Voltair and Dickens were noted customers.

On my previous visits, the pub is always busy. There are several rooms and a full menu is served. Walking in the door, you'll notice it is one of darkest pubs you'll visit. Directly on the right is a tiny bar room with about six or eight seats in old, dark oak pews. There's also a coal burning stove to keep you warm and to continue darkening the wood.

I was so impressed with this tiny room on my first visit a few years earlier, that it inspired me to do a renovation of the second level at Stuff Yer Face in New Jersey. My restaurant had two rooms upstairs, about 15 x 15 each with oak wainscoting and oak flooring. It now resembles a London Pub that we call the Upstairs Pub. I sketched out the plans while sitting in this very room here at the Ye Olde Cheshire Cheese with a pint of Sam Smith Xtra stout.

Looking to the left after entering is a small dining room measuring about 15 x 15. Here we get lucky and were able to sit at a small table. The walls of the room are decorated with old portraits, and there is a fireplace with a sign which suggests no smoking. The Cheshire Cheese has waiter service. The food is old style and we order a stuffed loin of pork plate. As a side, we had an opportunity to taste Bubbles and Squeak. I had heard of this dish before, but never had a chance to taste it. The name, Bubbles and Squeak, hints at what it may be. I can best describe it as mash potatoes with shredded cabbage mixed in. The food was fantastic, and paired nicely with the Sam Smith Xtra stout.

Our visit to London is over. We were surprised in the morning with a dusting of snow on the streets. As we rode in a taxi to Victoria Station, we passed Buckingham Palace with snow covering the golden gates. A beautiful, peaceful, feeling.

London to us was like Manhattan on steroids. There was a very fast pace on the streets, but life in the pubs slows down. People take the time to talk to one another and enjoy a pint.

We couldn't help but notice that they also enjoy their cigarettes. I don't want to keep mentioning it, but the smoke and the air was horrible, you need to be warned. So many people crammed into so little space and the majority of them smoking. I don't think that if I lived here that I would get to a pub each day. I might have to stay at home, but then that would defeat the purpose of the pub. Let's wish the pub goers good luck with their no smoking law that is about to start up.

England has perfected the pub atmosphere and design. The pubs are steeped with history. Their congeniality, their design, and the beers will draw people in for years to come. Pubs like the Ye Olde Cheshire Cheese, never seem to change. Soon, they will have to make a change to their British Monarch plaque outside their pub entrance, indicating a change in the Monarchy, but I'm sure no changes will be made inside the pub.

BAVARIA, GERMANY
and BOHEMIA, CZECH REPUBLIC

I'm sitting here in Florida, wishing I had a favorite pub to go to today. But, I don't. I'm thinking of Klosterbrau in Bamberg, Germany which I visited just a year and a half ago, or Kloster Andechs in Southern Bavaria near the Alps. If my favorite pub were here in Florida, it would have delicious, simple pub food, great tasting and uncomplicated fresh beer, and a friendly staff and fellow customers. It seems Southern Florida is stuck in that plain beer mode. If you ask a bartender "what's on tap?", the response is the long winded, "Bud, Bud light, Coors, Coors light, Miller, Miller Lite, Corona, Corona light, and Guinness". Give me a break. The bottled beer list doesn't have much more variety, but it may have a sprinkling of other "exotic" choices, if they can find any of them in their beer cooler.

    I could go to Yard House, a small chain that started in California. They boast about their 70 or so beers on tap. A pretty good selection, usually tasting fresh, but none of those "great" beers. It's a modern looking place with lots of stainless steel piping. However, for me, the food doesn't match the beers. The menu has an Asian flair to it. The food tastes great, but it's just not beer food. I could go to the local "Irish Pub", and they offer Chimay Blue by the bottle, but the staff is surprised when I order it, so it is a bit of a turn off. There is an authentic British Pub that I like, but it is almost a 45 minute drive away. It's not convenient.

    I suppose I am getting a bit spoiled now with enjoying more travels for beer lately. I'm thinking about those delicious, chewy, dark, smooth, malty, beers of

Bamberg along side a plate of grilled bratwurst and a side of sauerkraut. Or, those super thirst-quenching weisse beers of Bavaria with a freshly baked, giant, salted pretzel. Just think of this, no matter how good a Pilsner Urquell tastes here from the bottle or the tap, it must be better in it's own backyard, don't you think? How do you feel after traveling across the ocean from the USA to Europe? A little tired, a little haggard, not quite yourself? Imagine the beer sitting in the hull of a ship for a few weeks. It can't be any good for the taste. The beer at it's source has flavors that explode in your mouth. The beers are served along with typical beer cuisine that perfectly matches.

I have a feeling, or a need, to live in Germany and experience what life would be like with fresh German beer, food and music available all the time. I have a need to go to the source of some of the world's great beers. Drinking them fresh where they are brewed, and eating the perfect food that has been served with beer for centuries. Maybe I need three weeks in Germany and the Czech Republic, more specifically Bavaria and Bohemia.

When I planned this trip, the timing of it meant that I would miss the season's opening home game of the New York Yankees. That hasn't happened to me in 25 years! Opening Day is a great social event for a dedicated fan, but I'm determined to satisfy my yearnings for Europe. I love my Yankees, but I'm tired of going there and eating cold hot dogs and drinking a warm Silver Bullet beer. It isn't cheap either at $6.75 for 20 ounces! It seems that this is a great example of what we have done here in America to ruin some great traditions taught to us by our immigrant ancestors. Cold hotdogs served with warm tasteless beer, instead of fresh off the grill homemade sausages served with a 400 year old traditionally brewed beer.

I need some authentic beer culture! A place where society has a high regard for its brewing, art, history and cuisine. A society, which believes the brewery, is part of the foundation of the village, and where the brewer is as important as the blacksmith, or the carpenter, or the banker, or the weaver. To me, it seems that in Bavaria and Bohemia, life is still that old style way. There, typically you will find the hometown brewery still in operation like a couple of hundred years ago. What would it be like to live where beer is included in the culture? Where the service or drinking of beer is not frowned upon, but accepted as part of the daily life. Everywhere you turn in Bavaria there seems to be a bier garten. No major event takes place in Germany without a band or a bier garten being set up.

On the Internet, I came across an organization in Germany named the Private Braugasthof. They have a terrific website and a well-designed brochure in both English and Deutsch. The members have three things in common. First, they are all small to medium sized family operations. Second, they run their own brewery. Third, they operate a closely connected guesthouse or hotel. The group's purpose is to revive and preserve the historical unity of brewer and innkeeper. The more than fifty members are each an integral part of the village or town in which they are situated. Looking through the brochure, I notice that some are rustic and small, and others are large and more modern. The owners care about their beer, the food served, and the comfort of their guests.

This is just what I want to seek out! How perfect. I want to go to the source for some of the world's best beers and food. I will include in my newest travels for beer some Brauereigasthofs and a few additional stops at major breweries. Maybe going to the source will quench my thirst for that beer culture and great tasting fresh beer that I really desire.

I began to put together an itinerary of two weeks in Bavaria and one week in Bohemia! Including:

Bamberg, and their delicious brown lagers from the
   ten local breweries
Freising, home of Weihenstephan beers, which claims
   to be the oldest brewery in the world since 1040
Munich, just in time for Starkbeirzeit, or Strong Beer
   Festival serving up their doppelbocks
Aying, home of Ayinger Hotel and their award
   winning beers
Winklerbrau Private Braueriegasthof brewing
   since 1437
Eck Private Braueriegasthof which has been
   brewing since 1462
Kelheim and Kloster Weltenburg which has been
   brewing since 1050
Regensburg home to our favorite 700 year old
   wurst stand
Passau, a 2000 year old city where three major
   rivers converge
Ceske Budjevice, home of the original
   Budweiser beers
Prague, that ornate city saved from both
   World Wars and home to great brew pubs
Pilsen, where Pilsner Urquell was the first
   pilsner brewed on earth
Nuremberg, a city linked to the criminal trials of WWII, and
   home to some great beer cellars
Frankfurt, a modern city with a good old town

   While doing the planning and the research for the trip, I realize that this time in March will be Strong Beer Season in Germany. It is a time of year when Christians observe Lent with fasting. The brewers of the area produce their most nourishing beers for sustenance.

Bavaria, think of it as a state of Germany, lies in the Southeast corner of the country. It borders with Switzerland and Austria in the South and the Czech Republic in the East. A picturesque area which Americans imagine all of Germany to look like, especially during Christmas season. Bavaria lost its independence and became a part of Germany in 1918 after World War I. It's capital is Munich, where Hitler rose to power before World War II. Most of Munich was destroyed during the war, but has been rebuilt and revitalized. If Bavaria was considered a country by itself, Bavarians would win the drinking award for consuming the most beer per capita and also the award for the most breweries per capita.

Of course, the Czechs maintain the distinction for the most beer consumed per capita, usually, with an emphasis on the people of Bohemia. Bohemia is located in the Western part of the Czech Republic, which shares a mountainous border with Germany. Conflicts are historical within this area between the two nations. Hitler was practically given the area by the English and the French in 1938 to avoid a larger conflict later. How insulted were the Czechs? After WWII and Communist rule, in 1993 Czechoslovakia peacefully divided into two nations, the Czech Republic and Slovakia. Within the area of Bohemia is where the first pilsner beer, or gold color beer was brewed. Pilsner Urquell of course, in the city of Pilsen in 1842.

What an area of the world for beer exploration!? Nina and I leave in early March, ready for any kind of weather with our carry-on luggage. How do we do it? We think practical, color coordinate, use layering, plan on doing laundry, and don't plan on dressing to the nines! The flight from the New York area to Frankfurt is about 3800 miles and seven hours. We'll be ready to go when we arrive. It will be 3am for our body clock, but 9am for our watch. No time for naps or sleeping. We check in at our hotel and grab our pub list!

Our first stop was Bamberg. Located about 30 minutes by train North of Nurnberg, it was two hours by train from the Frankfurt airport. The brewing tradition in Bamberg dates back almost 900 years, if monasteries are considered as the first breweries. As early as in the 12th Century, beer from Bamberg was being exported. Bamberg has ten breweries within the city limits, all within walking distance of each other. The population is just over 70,000, so that is one brewery for each of its 7000 people! In Bavaria, the locals consider beer as the fifth element along with earth, water, air and fire.

We arrive in Bamberg at lunchtime. It was a sunny cool day and most of the people of Bamberg were sunning themselves in an outdoor café. These cafés weren't on our list of pub stops, but they were hard to resist. We pick the brightest one alongside a fountain. This particular café supplied flannel blankets in case you got a chill. My first beer, craved for several months in Florida, was the Aecht Schelenkerla rauchbier. The famous smoked beer they have been brewing since 1678. If you like smoked meat or cheese, you will love this beer. Dark brown, tan head and a good dose of smoke. The smoke doesn't knock you over, but it is obviously there. It might wear you down, but you have to admit, at least one of these beers is delicious. Selecting what to eat or just munch on here is easy, always some sort of sausage. We are content after just a few minutes and ready to go to work and taste some incredible beers.

We set out in the direction of Klosterbrau, a favorite of ours from a previous visit. It's amazing how our memory works, we knew exactly which streets to walk down. We even figured out a short cut to get there. We both were tasting the Schwarzla before we got there! Just as we remembered it, a dark alley entryway, the first door on the right leads into the gastube, a small bar room. It's a big solid wood door, that you would not open unless you knew something from before. No changes here. No changes here since probably 1533 when it started. We wished we could have sat outside on this sunny day, but construction was happening next door. We glance at the menu and select a braun bier and a schwarzla bier.

The braun is 5.7% full of flavor, thick mouth feel, buttery caramel hints, and a gold amber color. It leaves me with a thirst for more. The Schwarzla, or black beer, is 4.9%, smells roasty and coffee-like, robust in flavor, and has a less thick mouth feel. Both beers are very satisfying, and remind me of why I wanted to visit again. I love this place. I have only sat in one of the three rooms, and have never seen it busy, but it is always contenting.

As I slip away for my first visit to the pissort, a new customer walks into the gastube. Nina quickly recognizes him as someone we met on our last visit, Igon. He also recognizes her, even though my absence is obvious. Igon was a character we met on our last visit to Klosterbrau who tells us he has links to Hitler's mom. He is a daily regular here, usually with his dog, but the dog is on Holiday, as Igon explains. We share a beer with him, and he offers to guide us around the town of Bamberg. We are unsure, because we do have our agenda to stick to. Ten breweries in two afternoons is no easy task, no time for messing around. We next sample the Bock bier, a hefty 7% brewed for the strong beer season. It was more bubbly than I anticipated, but it had a beautiful rich gold color, strong hop flavor and a full head. Just as rewarding as the other brews here.

As in Rome, there are seven hills that make up the landscape of Bamberg. We finish up at Klosterbrau, and want to venture out to see more. We stay on the same side of the river Danube and walk uphill to find our next stop, the brewery Greifenklau. On our way we pass signs for bierkellers. They are not really beer cellars, but biergartens. Years ago, caves were dug in the sandstone for the storage and fermenting of the lagers. To help keep the cellars cool in the summer, chestnut trees were planted above the cellars. In Bamberg during the summer months, they drink outside, directly over the real underground kellers, under those nice shady trees. They were closed today, a little too early in the season, but I could imagine the picturesque sights from the benches. After a lengthy walk, we come across Greifenklau, which has been brewing since 1719. It's not a special looking place, but it seems this is where most tourists don't venture to.

Inside we find wood paneling to seven feet above the floor, with coat hooks at the top, and several large tables with benches. The ceiling is wood planked and decorated with hops. A couple of tables have some older gents seated and playing cards. Our beer selections are limited to weisse or pils. We order one of each.

The weisse was a typical citrusy, spicy, and clove tasting. The pils was amber gold in color, good amount of hops, and a perfect malt balance. The pils seemed to have no head, but the pils at the other table had a full head. Should they give the flat beer to the tourist? We watch them pour the beers from our seats. They seem to fill the glass halfway with beer, then they insert into the beer what looks like a small electric prod. Immediately, the head on the beer begins to climb inside the glass! When the head reaches the top of the glass, they pull the prod out of the glass. We didn't like that voodoo beer pour and left. Looking back, I suppose we should have asked them about that procedure.

We have a long walk back to the hotel area and it is getting dark now. Directly across the street from our hotel is the brewery Ambrausianum. The newest brewery in town and bills itself as the first guesthouse and brewery in Bamberg. The copper tanks are on display, a small bar, and green plants are hanging. We get a warm pretzel, which makes us happy. The beers, helles and dunkel, are unfiltered here. The dunkel was delicious. Smooth, not too sweet, with a pretty, burnt orange brown color. We're finished for the night, we even spilled a beer!

We start the next day refreshed and start walking towards the Franconian Beer Museum near St. Michaelsberg Church. It's a good walk, uphill, of course. It's a pretty day. Neither of us mind the walk. We follow signs to the museum, easily found, but it's closed for the season. This Spring trip is going to find us early by a couple of days or weeks, for the seasonal openning of several places and events. No problem, the view is good from up here looking down on the city. We change our plans, and decide to cross the river and visit the breweries on the other side.

On the way we stop at Wirsthaus Zum Sternla, which means Tavern Sternla. It's been in existence since 1380. We grab the last table available for lunch. To drink, we ordered an Eine Bamberger Weisse and a St. Michaelsberg dunkel. The weisse was a straw gold color, with a bright white head, and just a hint of clove. Very refreshing. The dunkel was brewed by Maisel Brau, and was a good session beer. It was dark brown, smooth, light, and just a hint of smoke in the finish. Our server was very friendly and quick. To eat, we devoured an "ofenfrischer schweinkrustenbraten", an oven fresh, crusty pork fillet. It was served with a smoked beer sauce, that was just fantastic. Perfect succulent pork with a skin crust baked crispy. We could have camped out here today, but we have work to do. This was definitely a local place.

We are walking towards the East on the North side of Bamberg headed in the direction of three breweries. The Main-Danube Canal seems to slice the city North and South. The first brewery that we come across is Keesmann Brau. Keesmann has been brewing since 1867. The stuberl is a bright room with stained glass windows, wooden benches and tables. It's a cozy, pleasant room to sit in.

Since it is Strong Beer season here in Bavaria we have our eyes open at each brewery for any doppelbocks. Keesmann is offering its Josephi Bock. Nina goes for it. It has a deep orange color, mild clove taste, and tangy, with a long finish of hops. I selected the Herren Pils. The beer mat boasts "edel herb" which I interpret to mean noble herb, meaning the most flavorful hops. It has a light gold color, slightly floral, and a pleasant balance of the hops and malt. We also get excited because we can grab a pretzel off the stick sitting on the table. If it's early in the day they are usually tasty and less than a Euro each. We drink a few beers here.

Diagonally across the street from Keesmann is Mahr's Brau. Mahr's is first mentioned in any writings in 1602, and has been in the Mahr's family since 1895. When you first walk under the tall gate, your eyes go directly to the brewery's yard where thousands of kegs and bottle cases are sitting. Upon entering the drinking area, the main hallway has storage facilities for steins that the locals use. This must be a good drinking place! The stuberl is small, warm and cozy with a fireplace. We order Weisse bock and a sternen-helles.

The weisse bock has a great logo on the glass with a goat. Bock, is also a word meaning goat. The beer is dark with a tan head, bubbly, sweet, malty, medium clove, and delicious. It seems the Sternen helles is the result of several brewers' efforts to commemorate the 1000 year jubilee of the Bamberger Diocese. Imagine 1007-2007 for the church of Bamberg! Between the local water, the hops, and the malt this beer is just great. Deep gold color, with a soft mouth feel, it has a great taste.

We have walked a good number of miles today, so we decide not to go further East to find Maisel Brau, and instead head back towards old town and the hotel. Around the corner from the hotel is the famous Schlenkerla Brau, famous for its worldly smoked beer. First mentioned in 1405, and now run by the Trum family in their 6th generation. According to their website, "Schlenkern" is an old German expression for not walking straight (just as a drunken person does). Allegedly one of the former brewers had a funny way of walking due to an accident (or maybe due to the beer), and so he was called the "Schlenkerla". After a while, the residents of Bamberg also called the tavern "Schlenkerla".

Smokebeer from Schlenkerla is a dark, aromatic, bottom fermented beer with an alcohol content of 5.1 %. The beers are still tapped from the wooden barrel. Smoked beer is called "rauchbier" in German. How does the beer get its smoked flavor? According to their website, "green malt always had to be dried (kilned). In the past, besides the usage of the sun's rays (which was quite difficult in Europe) there was only one way to achieve this: drying it over an open fire. Thus, it was unavoidable that smoke penetrated the malt and gave it a smoky flavor. Technical developments over the centuries made it possible to produce malt without an open fire, thus without a smoky taste. Original Schlenkerla Smokebeer has preserved that old tradition of smoking the malt. Therefore you are, in effect, having a little piece of the past with every swallow."

The pub is a great place to visit. Many different connected rooms, all woodsy and cozy. The room we sit in is bright from the windows. The room seems filled with older residents. No young people in here. I wonder if the smoked flavor is more liked by the aged palate. On the table is a display for the Fastenbier, the Lenten beer that we are looking for. To us it tastes less smoky than the original Schlenkerla, a tad sweeter, and has a beautiful orange brown color.

It's time to eat some kind of dinner. We know the food and beer at Ambrausianum is great and close, so we head on over for our second dinner there. We spill another beer there that night, so off to bed we go. I'm sorry to say that we ended two nights at Ambrausianum and never really got to fully enjoy their beers. We should have made it a first stop on one of the days.

The next day is a travel day. We need to catch a train to Munich. It's only about an hour and a half away. Munich will be the site of two Strong Beer Festivals, for which we have reserved seats. We want to get to Munich around noon, check into the hotel, drop off our bags, and then take the S-bahn to Freising. Why Freising? Because that is where Weihenstephan is located.

Freising, just 20 miles North of Munich, is one of Bavaria's oldest towns, and it was founded in the 8th Century. By the 12th Century, under Bishop Otto von Freising, the area had begun a spiritual and cultural boom. Freising, however, was caught in a bitter rivalry with Munich that had repercussions lasting from the 12th Century until the beginning of the 19th Century. Bishop Otto owned a profitable toll bridge over the Isar River until 1156 when Henry the Lion destroyed it and built his own bridge, wrestling control of the lucrative salt route from the bishop and founding his settlement, München. It was Freising that went into decline then as Munich prospered.

Nearly one thousand years ago Weihenstephan was the monastery brewery of the Benedictine monks. It is now The Bavarian State Brewery Weihenstephan and surrounded by the comparatively very young Weihenstephan Science Centre of the Technical University of Munich. In 1040, beer brewing officially began at Weihenstephan. That year Abbot Arnold succeeded in obtaining from the City of Freising a license to brew and sell beer. That hour marked the birth of the Weihenstephan Monastery Brewery. At the doorsteps of the Weihenstephan Monastery, in the year 1516, Duke Wilhelm II of Bavaria issued the Bavarian Beer Purity Law, the Rheinheitsgebot. Since then and still today, only barley, hops and water are to be used in Bavarian beer. He thus founded the world reputation of Bavarian beer.

We have a crude map to get us from the train station to Weihenstephan. It's a clear sunny, cool day and looks as if we have about a half hour walk. Quickly, we are a little fooled by a church sitting high above us on a hill, thinking this was Weihenstephan. However, being confident in our map reading it seems to be in the wrong place. So, we head out on our hike to the brewery. The hike was probably three miles in total, almost an hour. The route is not really marked well and soon we found ourselves in the middle of a courtyard filled with students from the Technological University. There was a terrific view above the city, but where is the stuberl? We can see stacks of empty kegs and we just wander around. Our noses take us in the right direction and we find the entrance.

It's a nice, woodsy place with several special rooms that are closed, but the main stuberl was open. Not too many people were there at 2pm. The room, with great views on one side, was filled with the typical large wood tables and chairs. We sat right in the middle, hoping to miss nothing. Since it is strong beer season, Nina notices the ad for Vitus on the table, the weizenbock of the season. She quickly orders one. I always start with the simplest of choices from the tap and began with the hefeweissbier. When it was delivered, I had to notice the brilliance of the yellow gold beer with the very white head. It tasted so fresh and thirst quenching it was a shock compared to what we drink at home. Nina's Vitus was a dark weisse, brewed for the season at 7.7%, which was slightly less cloudy than normal. Vitus is the patron saint of Beer Brewers. This beer was a Lenten special to help nourish and satisfy the body while fasting.

While enjoying our first selections, a local walks in, grabs a newspaper, and sits down in the chair next to me, even though ninety percent of the other chairs are available. Okay with me, but a little odd. He says no words to the waitress, but accepts a tall weisse beer. We prost each other and he starts to read his newspaper.

We're ready for round two. Nina goes for the Korbinian, a doppelbock. She's not messing around this afternoon. The walk up the hill must have made her thirsty. It's 7.4%, nice and dark, smooth and malty. Very delicious. I step it up to the traditional dunkel bier. Easy drinking, 5.3%, brown and flavorful. We are both happy with our beers and are amazed at the freshness in taste. We sit and enjoy the view of the hillside surrounding us. Our table companion has finished the paper, two glasses of weisse and is beginning to get frisky.

We try to speak to him, but he understands no English, and our German is not going to go too far with him. He gets up and brings us some Weihenstephan pamphlets from a drawer behind the bar. I begin to think that maybe he is someone special connected with the brewery. His beers just keep coming without even the slightest nod of the head. He starts to tell us stories about the beers and the area. He is very proud to live in Freising. He told us the interesting story of Korbinian the Bishop who rode into Freising on a donkey, slayed a big, bad bear and got a great beer named after him. I don't understand a word he is saying, but Nina seems to follow along like a good foreign movie.

He takes me outside on a deck, explains, and points out that all the hops and wheat are grown on those hillsides. He's a great tour guide. Our next beers are the dunkel hefeweissbiers. They are just 5.2%, caramel in color and have a taste that goes down easy. Our local guide, Klaus, has another one or two. He explains that after four beers he begins to feel drunk. Good for him, I have a buzz on and have made two trips to the pissort, he just sits at the table, talking, drinking, drinking, and talking!

Later we are all drinking the regular hefeweisse and he gives us an important prosting tip: don't clang together the bowls of the weisse glass, instead tap the more solid bottoms together. Good tip at this point. It's time to leave though. We walk out together, he jumps on a little moped, and off he goes. Nina and I both make note of the fact that he never excused himself from the table while drinking six 20-ounce weisse beers. A mighty good session indeed. As for us, we begin our downhill hike back to the station.

About three quarters of the way there, we stopped off at a little Spaten pub. There was a cute happy woman behind the bar, which was filled with locals. This was the kind of place where everyone is shocked to see a stranger walk into their bar. That's no matter to us. We notice that Triumphator is on tap here. That's the strong beer from Lowenbrau for the season. We order two, the crowd knows it, and they seem comfortable with us. That's funny. The beer was just delicious. Now we know what to expect when we get to Munich for Strarkbierzeit. We are worried though about drinking this stuff in liter mugs!

Just what is Starkbierzeit? It's German for "strong beer festival," or "strong beer time". This is an event held every March in Munich and the surrounding areas. It's a season when the breweries bring out their most potent beverages, and beer halls throw some good festivals with lots of Bavarian entertainment and food. It's supposedly Oktoberfest without the tourists.

Bavaria is a stronghold for the Roman Catholics. The Paulaner Monks having actually founded Munich, participate in the observance of Lent. The Festival's roots go back to the Paulaner Monks who, according to legend, began making an extra-strength beer to sustain themselves during their Lenten fast. The beer, first brewed in the 17th Century, gained a word-of-mouth following. The townspeople called it Salvator. The flavors of the beer were popular and copied, and also honored with names ending in "ator". The Strong Beers are usually doppelbocks, strong bock beers coming in at around 7% alcohol.

We have reserved seats for the Strong Beer Festival at Augustiner Keller on Friday night and at Lowenbrau Keller for Saturday night. We are working hard! The new morning finds me a little foggy. It's a good thing we have been to Munich several times before, because I didn't feel like I was wasting the day away by wandering aimlessly. We did find our way to the Nyphemburg Castle. It was one of King Ludwig's homes in town. The tour was a great way to spend some relaxing time during the day.

At lunchtime, we go to Andechser am Dom, a pub serving the beers of Kloster Andechs. It is located along side the famous twin towered church, Frauenkirch. Nina and I have previously made a journey together to Kloster Andechs, located near the Alps, and we love their beers. They have been brewing beers since 1455. The sky is partly sunny, getting cold and the wind is kicking up. Inside all the tables are taken. We don't feel overly socialable this afternoon, and don't want to squeeze ourselves in. The tables outside have heaters standing near, so we grab a warm seat. Of course, Andechs is serving their Doppelbock dunkel for the season. We should have one. Two mugs were delivered that were so beautiful. The doppelbock is a dark brown beer, 7%, with a thick tan head. The beer smelled of malt, and had tastes of chocolate. We both said, "wow". No other way to describe it, it really picked us up for the afternoon.

The Andechs beer mat has a slogan "Genuss fur leib and seele" which translates to "Enjoyment for the body & soul". They got that right. That is just what we came looking for here in Germany. Not "Tastes great, less filling"! We ordered food for lunch and had more enjoyment for our bodies. Chive infused mash potatoes, sauerkraut, and of course sausage. Why leave this spot? We were warm under our heater and the beer is perfect. Oh yeah, Strong Beer Festival in a couple of hours.

I have to admit I was a little nervous walking over to Augustiner Keller that evening. We had six o'clock reservations, but really no idea of what to expect as far as the event went. Other tour notes that I had read, mentioned that tourists usually didn't go to this festival as they do for Oktoberfest. The international flair of Oktoberfest makes it easier to find other festival rookies. This Strong Beer Festival may be a large group of professionals drinking liter mugs of 7% sweet beer. We arrive just ten minutes early and no one is seated in the special festival room. We grab a quick liter of helles before going in. Of course, the Germans show up exactly on time at six, and the seats quickly fill up.

We are escorted to our seats. The room is large, decorated with banners, and a band is already playing. Our table mates are a group of six guys in their fifties. We can order food, but we hold off and go for the Maximator. Maximator is Augustiner's version of the Strong Bier, the only beer available tonight. It's delivered in liter mugs of course. Liters are okay at Oktoberfest with the easy to drink, low alcohol percentage helles beer, but the doppelbock? The last thing I wrote in my journal that evening was that the Maximator was a strong beer, dark brown in color, malty, with a thin mouthfeel, not as satisfying as the Andechers. My memories are vague for that night, remembering only the crazy band and dancing with Nina. Why, at all the beer festivals in Germany, do they crave John Denver's *Take Me*

Home Country Road? We eventually partied with our table mates, and they insisted that I meet them early the next morning to play soccer with them. What are you crazy? Nina tells me we took a cab ride home that night.

The next evening rolled around real quick. We are meeting friends that we had met at an Oktoberfest a year and a half earlier. They live in Landshut, and they will meet us at the front door to the Lowenbrau Keller on Nyphemburger Strasse. Meeting up with people in Germany is easy, because like me, they are always on time. As we approach the keller, we notice that outside the main entrance a whole oxen is roasting on a spigot. The cook is shaving the meat off the bones for tonight's service. Smells and looks great. We meet our friends, Jurgen, Nicole, and Sebastian. Jurgen did some negotiating and arranged for all of us to sit together. Nina and I had been to Lowenbrau several times for lunch before this visit. However, we had never seen the room that we were escorted to. Very large, upstairs, it probably sat a thousand people. It was very nicely decorated, and the band was ready to play.

The schedule for the night included beer drinking, band playing, special dance acts, stone lifting contests for the strong men, a beauty contest for the pretty girls, traditional dancing, yodeling, wood chopping and eating. Lowenbrau offered several of their beers, but we were there for the Strong Beer, Triumphator. Again served in liter mugs, it was dark and toasty, better tasting than the Maximator, with a thicker mouthfeel. Nina and I agreed that the Andechs doppelbock was still the best.

Lowenbrau did a great job with the evening. There was never a dull moment with something live going on at all times. Lots of prosting here. The heavy stone-lifting contest was fun to watch. Big boys lifting round stones that must have weighed 300 pounds. I had my own contest at the table. Sebastian challenged me to a mug-lifting contest. Not lifting above your head, but held with your arm straight out perpendicular from your chest. That's not too easy with a full liter. This being my second Strong beer Festival in two days, I was more experienced and won! I didn't win anything except bragging rights to my Bavarian Bock Babe. That is Nina's new nickname.

The next day is another travel day. I planned for a day of rest at the Ayinger Brauereigasthof in Aying. It's just about 30 minutes South of Munich via the S-bahn. Looking at the website it seems to be high-end with saunas and pools and a fancy restaurant. A day of recovery for us. Ayinger uses a slogan on their advertising which states "edite bierkultur geniessen" which translates to "enjoy real beer culture". That's what we're looking for, and the goal of our trip! Ayinger beers are also high end, winning awards annually. I have always loved their version of their Oktoberfest bier, although, they are not allowed to sell it at the actual Oktoberfest fairgrounds. Remember, only the original six Munich brewers can pour beer at the Fest.

The Internet directions say to take the S-bahn to Aying, follow the signs and walk 300 meters to the hotel. Sounds easy, but we couldn't understand the first sign that we found. Maybe, it was all the Strong Beer that we drank during the last three days that confused us. We see a dozen people get off the train with us, walking together in the same direction, so we decide to follow them. We figure all roads lead to Ayinger beer. Well, the 300 meters must have been 600, and about four unmarked turns gets us to the front of the hotel. It's a beautiful place from the outside, with a large Maypole standing outside the front door. A Maypole is a tall wooden post, festively decorated, that traditionally represents a villages' communal center. As we step inside the Inn, it begins to snow outside. The good weather we enjoyed for the first week was probably coming to an end.

The Ayinger Inn was first referred to in 1385, in an official documentation as a "tavern and place of jurisdiction". The Ayinger Brewery is privately owned, where Bavarian beer culture has been alive and well since 1878. They are proud to know how to brew the very best beers using old beer traditions along with the latest ecological knowledge. The brewery and inn are the centerpoint of the sleepy town of Aying.

Within the Gasthof are two different restaurants, one more formal than the other, where some of the food is prepared using the beers. The restaurant room was very cozy with a fire burning on this quiet, snowy night. Wooden booths with padded seats, low hanging light fixtures, historical photos on the walls, and glass windows made of bottle bottoms.

And, of course, there are the beers. Where do we start? The Jahrhundert Bier was first brewed in 1978 to celebrate the 100th anniversary of the brewery. At 5.5%, it has a golden-yellow color with a slightly flowery yeast flavor, and honey aroma. It tastes a little spicy and is full-bodied in the initial taste. A good beer to start the evening.

The glimmering, light-yellow Ayinger Pils, 5%, has the fragrance of aromatic hops from the "Hallertau" region of Bavaria. The beer is highly fermented and therefore smooth on the initial taste sensation, but also mild and sparkling in body. The pils is accentuated by the floweriness of the hops aroma and has a more pronounced bitterness upon swallowing.

Nina's favorite is the Celebrator doppelbock, 6.7%, another strong beer that has a dominant malty taste. The beer is a very dark brown with a very slight red tone, a good strong head and malty fragrance. There are hints of coffee in the aftertaste.

Liebhard's Kellerbier, 4.9% alcohol, is brewed in commemoration of the good old times and in honor of the brewery's founder, Johann Liebhard. The special feature of the "Kellerbier" is the fine yeasty cloudiness and the pleasantly bitter taste. As it is bottled unfiltered, many of the natural protein, yeast and hop elements remain contained in the beer. Consequently, it retains its original character. Furthermore, the vitamin and mineral-rich yeast also provides a significant contribution to the nutritional requirements of good health.

A pleasant surprise for us during dinner was the appearance of Angela Inzelkammer. Mrs. Inzelkammer, along with her husband Franz, are the owners of Ayinger Brewery. At first she appeared very businesslike in her red suit, but quickly showed her social mood and visited her dining guests at each table. There were probably a dozen tables for her to visit and she spent at least five or ten minutes at each. That's not real easy to do.

We recognized her because there are photos of all the employees hanging on the walls of the inn. It reminded me of Stuff Yer Face Restaurant where we showcase almost everyone who has worked at the restaurant in the last 30 years. She approached our table with a warm welcoming smile and spoke English very well. Our conversation wasn't just small talk, as she was genuinely interested in finding out who we were and where we were from.

When I told her about Stuff Yer Face, she related a story of her daughter's recent visit to the United States. It seems that her children are involved in the business and that she was visiting Ayinger customers. Mrs. Inzelkammer added that it was her son's turn to visit the States this year. I expressed an interest in meeting her son at Stuff Yer Face during his visit. She asked that I leave my business card for her. Maybe Stuff Yer Face can return the hospitality.

The Ayinger beers win many awards. In the July 2005 issue of *Men's Journal* there was an editor's list of the top eight beers of the world. Celebrator doppelbock was selected as the dark beer, Brau Weisse was selected as the Summer weisse beer, and the Jahrhundert lager received an honorable mention. That is an impressive sweep of categories by Ayinger!

It is a Tuesday morning and we took a short walk from the inn to the Ayinger Brewery. It is set in the middle of an open field. The brewery was closed for tours on Tuesdays, but we decided to test the door anyway. It opened and we stood in the middle of the copper brewing vessels. No security here, but we were greeted by a gent who seemed a little upset with us. We told him we were staying at the Inn and he quickly changed his demeanor. Being very friendly, he explains that there were no private tours today, but he had a French guided group tour in a few minutes and that we were welcome to join them. It would be nice to see the operation, but we didn't understand any French, so we declined. He looked at his watch and quickly gave us a personal ten-minute tour, in English. That was really nice of him.

When his French group arrived, he suggested for us to go upstairs to the pub and gift shop to look around. We climbed two flights of stairs and walked into an excellent pub. The tables and chairs, and small bar, were surrounded by three walls of glass, which opened up to the fields and hillsides around. We wished it were open and that we could have an afternoon session here. It was beginning to snow again, and we have travel plans today.

Our plans today include the S-bahn back to Munich, and then a train to Regensburg to rent a car. Then we'll drive to our next Braugasthof in Legenfield, the Winkler Brau. Because of our visit to the Ayinger Brewery we are several hours behind schedule and our car pick up. When checking out of the Inn we ask the desk clerk, Alex, to call the car rental people and notify them that we'll be late. Luckily, we decided to do this, because he found out that our rental office had closed for business, last week! Alex really helped us out and found us another car locally. The new plans made us drive a couple of extra hours, instead of taking the train. But, it all worked out and soon we were on the road, driving in snow flurries, to our next stop.

Winkler Braustuberl is located between Regensburg and Bamberg just off the A3 highway. It is run by two families the Winklers and Bohms, and has been a Winkler family tradition since 1428. Imagine a property in your family for more than five hundred years! The drive was easy and scenic through the Hallertau hop region. It was early in the growing season, but we could see miles of large posts connected with holding wires for the hops to grow on. It's not too long now, for the hops to grow, and for the harvest. Maybe that's another idea for a trip? There was a large parking area and a beautiful rustic inn waiting for us when we arrived. The flurries were changing to a more steady snowfall and it looks like we arrived just in time.

To check in, we had to walk through the main stuberl, which is very woodsy and has a wood stove. It seemed crowded for this time of day, and with business people. Perfect. There are fifty-five rooms and ours was large, in a Bavarian style, and very clean. Not wasting any time, we head back down to the stuberl. The snow is heavy now and we aren't going anywhere else. The inn has a nice restaurant for dinner later. Nina's first beer was the Kupfer spezial, with kupfer meaning copper. It was smooth, mildly sour and reminded her of the London beers. That means she doesn't like it. I tasted the Hefe-Pils, a style that I had never heard of before. It was a pilsner with the yeast still in the bottle. At 4.8%, it was very delicious, good session beer, slightly cloudy, hoppy, and a nice yellow gold color. The foamy head was long lasting. Very good. So on this trip I have learned that a hefe-pils, keller bier, and zwickel are all about the same, straight from the barrel, unfiltered and unpasteurized. The way beer should be. They don't have a long shelf life, but they are delicious and natural.

We move to the restaurant and sample the Winkler export and Martini Trunpf beers. Nina tasted the export, which had an auburn color and a long sour finish. There will be no second for her. The Trunpf had a nice golden brown color, a good average dunkel, but no second was needed of this either. The winner of the group was the hefepils. For dinner we had some great cheeses, including a brie with juniper berries in it, some really dark tasty bread, and a fish stock based beet soup. Both dishes were delicious.

The snow was heavy now, with about three inches on the ground. We finished the night with a walk around the little village in the snow.

The staff members of Winkler Brau were all very congenial. We even came bearing gifts for Mr. Bohm. It seems our desk clerk at Ayinger Inn, Alex, knows him. He sent with us, a six-pack of Ayinger beers, along with a note asking Mr. Bohm to "taste some of Germany's finest beers". It was a good joke, and the gift of the beers was appreciated.

Today we must drive South and East an hour or so to Brauerei Gasthof Eck in Bobrach. Since we were driving past Regensburg we decided to stop for lunch. Regensburg is a beautiful, friendly, authentic medieval town complete with winding alleys. From a previous visit, we remember this great wurst restaurant sitting along side the Danube River. The Wurstkuchl claims to be the oldest bratwurst restaurant in the world. The wurststube is 500 years old and sits next to the Old Stone Bridge, built in 1200. Napolean once rode across this bridge, and it's the only bridge that he did not destroy here in Regensburg. They have a secret recipe for their pork sausages that are grilled over a charcoal grill. The sauerkraut is fermented in the cellar and the mustard is homemade. There are seats for 100 sausage eaters outside, just twenty feet from the Danube. They open at 8am!

Our favorite brauerei-gaststatte in Regensburg is Kneitinger. They have been brewing since 1530. The beers on the menu include, the edel-pils, export Dunkel, and Bock. All three are brewed to the traditional specifications and great representations of each style. The Bock had a nice orange tone to it with a good balance of malt and hops. The Dunkel was our favorite, malty, smooth and a never-ending tan head. They have a comfortable indoor biergarten with a glass roof.

Our overnight stop for the day, Brauerei Gasthof Eck, was very remote, almost a half-hour off the highway. The route was scenic though, with lots of rolling hills. We are now close to the Czech border. When we arrive, we find several rustic buildings and no cars in the parking lot. We had to find the brewer to get the room key, which was fine with us, but we didn't get an invite for a quick tour. There has been a brewery at this location since 1462. We find out that the stuberl is closed today, until 5pm so we have a couple of hours to fill.

Our room is very rustic and laden with the smell of tobacco. We should have changed rooms, but we didn't. It was snowing again. We opened the windows and turned up the heat. We start to walk the property and found a Schnapps Museum for Penninger Schnaps. It was very interesting, had an active still, and lots of old equipment on display. Of course, there was a tasting room. The employee was very generous with her free tastes. When we explained that we were guests here and not driving, I thought we would never get out alive. We tasted some great bier schnapps and bought some bottles to return home with, along with other fruit schnapps and glassware. Next door was a little shop to buy beer by the bottle. We purchased two to sample in our smelly room.

For an equivalent of $2.30 we purchased half liters of Bobracher pils and Wilderer Dunkel, two Eck specialties. The Pils had a large 1462 on the label, indicating the year Eck began brewing. It was 4.9%, light yellow in color, lightly hopped, and had a soft mouth feel. Quite good. Eck tells the story that this pils was first brewed in 1842, using a yeast culture smuggled by a Czech monk from the Weihenstephan Monastery. That story made the beer taste better to me. The Wilderer Dunkel was 5.5%, light auburn color, tan loose head, a little smoky, caramel and coffee flavors, and a thin pleasing mouth feel. There were no bitter after tastes.

When we arrive in the restaurant, we enter a building that reminds me of a ski lodge in Vermont. The dining room was very woodsy and only a few tables were filled. The other guests knew we were out of towners, and we knew that they knew. But we couldn't get a conversation started with anyone. The brewer was present at the stammtisch table. He seemed to have some trouble with the draft system that evening with the helles. When I could see it was finally pouring correctly, I asked for one. He served it, and said a quick hello. I mentioned to him that the beer was very tasty. Except for a quick, "danke", he was back to the stammtisch table. The helles was very good, just smooth, not too much hops, a great session beer for the stammtisch table. Nina and I finish an uneventful evening with a walk in the cold clear air around the hills and call it a night.

Breakfast was served in a really nice room with pillars and arched ceilings. This room would be a great drinking space. But, it's time to pack up the car, and drive towards Kelheim, near Regensburg. The goal is to get a room in Kelheim, but spend the day at Kloster Weltenburg, located just outside of town.

The hype that I read for Weltenburg is enticing. Their website tells me we'll find one of the most beautiful beer gardens in Bavaria located in the courtyard of the baroque monastery of Weltenburg, directly on the Danube. The best way to arrive is to take a boat from Kelheim through the romantic Danube gorge where you pass such beautiful sights like Ludwig I's Liberation Hall.

Founded around the year 600 A.D., on a picturesque peninsula on the Danube, Weltenburg is the oldest monastery in Bavaria. They claim to be "the oldest still existing" monastery brewery in the world, since 1050. Last week Nina and I were at Weihenstephan and they said they were "the oldest brewery" in the world since 1040. Which is the oldest? The key word here is monastery. Weihenstephan began as a monastic brewer but it is now state owned by Bavaria. Weltenburg is still a monastery.

We arrive in Kelheim and settle into our room within a personal residence, which was very nice. Again, the property was in the family for over 500 years. Doesn't anyone here change his or her occupation or sell their land? We can't help but notice Ludwig's Liberation Hall standing high above the city. It's about 144 years old and built in recognition of Germany's defeat of Napolean. Nina and I drove up to see it and were in awe by the size and grandeur of it. The views of the river and the city were outstanding. But we need to park the car, and get to the Klosterschenke of Weltenburg.

Our first disappointment with Weltenburg came when I was planning the trip. I found out that the ferry on the Danube to the Kloster did not start running for the season until the following week. We were one week too early for it. So we take a cab ride about seven miles and it cost $20. The cab driver was very friendly and gave us some tourist information on the area. He drops us off outside the Kloster. We notice that there are not too many people around. We ask, "Where is the beer garden?" He mentions it's too early in the season, but the stuberl inside is open.

I'm ready for some big beers, big food, and big fun here at this 1000 year old monastery! We look around and see a couple of doors. All the doors are locked. We look inside and see plenty of wooden tables and chairs and festive decorations. There are no people around. There is a sign on the door, and I recognize one word "geschlossen" which means closed. No way! The Internet said that it was open year round. Wrong.

We decide to walk the grounds and see the sights. The gorge on the Danube is very beautiful. The Baroque church is outstanding. The Trail of the Cross, is spiritually moving. But, where's the beer? We find ourselves back within the courtyard and we notice that the gift shop is open. We question the employee if anything is open, and she responds, "nine". I notice a stack of Weltenburg beer for sale and ask if it would be possible to purchase a bottle and drink on the premises. She says no problem, and opens two bottles of Dunkels for us and gives us a glass to use. We take the beers and glass outside in the biergarten and sit at a picnic table, under the chestnut trees, across from the entrance to the church. It was a little chilly, with the sun peaking out through the clouds.

We notice a gold statue of St. Peter standing above the door of the church and it glistens in the sun. Suddenly the sky opens up to a bright, deep blue. We open our beers and we pour an astonishing brown beer. After our first sips, we both agree it may be the best beer of the trip. It had a beautiful color, frothy head, and enticing malty smell. It tasted not sweet, not bitter, just a brown beer that tastes brown. The label read 4.7% and Baroque Dunkel. Those two beers under the chestnut trees went down so smooth. They made us yearn for more...but we couldn't...they were

CLOSED TODAY! That's okay, we had our experience at the monastery and we will remember it.

When leaving, we learned our third disappointment with Weltenburg. In three days, the Kloster was having their opening day Strong Beer Festival, the same day that the ferry would begin running. I'll just forget that I learned that. We call a cab and head back to Kelheim.

In the center of Kelheim, around the corner from our room, is a Weisses Brauhaus. The brauhaus is owned by the Schneider family, who brew those great weisse beers, including the original and Aventinus, the dark wheat beer. The exterior was very appealing with the setting sun glistening off the white/gray stones. The interior was very welcoming also. The Original weisse was the best I have ever tasted. So fresh and thirst quenching. Nina went with the Aventinus at 8%. Our waitress explained to us that the stark Aventinus, 12%, was not available on tap, only by the bottle. Either way, the ordering of the Aventinus got us the attention of the gents at the Stammtisch. The food was also excellent here. We shared a hot pretzel and an order of white sausage.

The next morning we need to return our rented BMW to Landshut, just one hour away near Regensburg.. What else would you rent in Bavaria? From there, we will catch a train to Passau. It's a two hour train ride, and we are very lucky to get the direct train when we arrive at the station.

Passau is near the intersection of Germany, Austria and the Czech Republic. When we exit the train station we both realize that the city has an Austrian flair to it, resembling Salzburg to us. The small narrow winding streets of Passau's well-known old town reflect its two thousand years of history. Passau, the city where the rivers Danube, Inn and Ilz meet, is a young, old city. You can walk along the Danube until a point where you stand at the meeting of the three rivers. Stand and look around, you will notice the high hilltops on two sides. On one side is the Castle Veste Oberhaus, which was built in 1219 by Bishops to control and tax the commerce on the rivers. On the Southern side is a baroque monastery, Mariahill. To reach Mariahill from the river's edge you need to walk up 321 covered "Pilgrim Steps". After the steep climb, great views of old Passau reward us.

Within old town Passau is the baroque Dom St. Stephen built around 500 AD which houses the world's largest cathedral pipe organ. It's clearly visible from anywhere on either side of the rivers with its green colored oxidized copper dome tops. We stumbled across the Romero Museum, which houses the remains of a Roman fort built around 250 AD, but was just recently found in 1974. There is lots of history here, and probably great beer.

Walking along the Danube I see many taverns to stop in, and many have signs up for Starkbierfests. Our first stop was at Peschl Brau. There has been a brewery at this site since 1259, and is the oldest brewery in Passau. The Peschl family has been operating the brewery since 1855 with five generations of the family.

It was a large building with an outdoor terrace facing the Danube, which on a warmer day would be jammed with tourists. Inside was a warm stuberl with great aromas of food. Most people around us seemed to be drinking the weisse beer. On our table was an advertisement for the Stephanus heller doppelbock at 7.5%. Seemed like a contradiction in terms to me, a light colored double bock I guess. We order two. They were served in beautiful half-liter ceramic steins with four-color artwork trimmed with gold highlights.

It is difficult to see the color of the beer in the ceramic stein before we take our first sip. There were no strong malty aromas, but the taste was slightly sweet with either hints of maple or honey, very smooth, slightly spicy, and creamy with a soft rounded mouth feel. When the foam settled we could see a deep gold color that was very entrancing. We both agreed this beer tasted great and was very drinkable.

The food was traditional and delicious, and the service was fast and efficient. We didn't need or want to try any of the other beers, so we just continued to order a couple more rounds of Stephanus. We were very content. When we paid the check we asked to purchase one of the steins to help us remember this great beer, but we were told it was not for sale. There was no persuading the server that day.

    A NOTE: Upon returning home from our travels for beer, I contacted the general information email address at the website for Peschl Brau. I asked if there was a way to purchase a Stephanus stein and have it shipped to the USA. I received a return email from Matthias Peschl stating that he would be coming to the US in one month and would bring a stein for me, and ship it while here.
    Wow! Thanks, Mr. Peschl. I'll be checking my mailbox.

During the next day we did the touristy things. We grabbed lunch and were able to taste some of the beers from Innstadt, a local brewery across the river from old town. The hefe-weisse and the dunkel weisse were very commendable and were a perfect match with the sausages.

    Today was my birthday. We wanted to find somewhere special to spend the evening having dinner and a couple of beers. Surprisingly, across the street from our hotel was Stifts Keller and Bier Stuberl. It didn't look like much from the outside, but the night before we did a little snooping and got interested in trying it. Behind the front stuberl, next to the kitchen, and through some dark wood doors, was a stone staircase. Peering down the staircase you could see candles in the darkness, and candles on each step.

    When you reach the bottom of the stairs you enter a vaulted stone ceiling room, with brick walls, heavy timbers, and candles almost everywhere. The air was filled with the aroma of burning wood from the fireplace. There was a small service bar. The chairs were of heavy wood that encircled your torso. We were the first to be seated so we selected a table where we could watch the action during the night. This also gave us some time to take some photos without bothering other diners. The high arched ceilings were 1000 years old and part of an old Franziskaner Kloster. It was opened for dining in 1969. This space was to be remembered.

Lowenbrau Triumphator, the strong beer for the season, was offered by the bottle. We liked it better than the "vom fass" version, or "from the tap", that we tasted in Munich. It seemed the flavors were fuller and there was less fizz than the tap version. It became the beer of choice for the evening. The room filled up quickly. The food was excellent. I started with a green colored, garlic soup that was flavored with chives and parsley and cream. For dinner, we enjoyed Ochenbrust with a creamed spinach sauce and veal medallions with cheese spatzle in a paprika sauce. The Triumphator worked well with both dishes.

Towards the end of the evening, we were about to leave half our beers when a chocolate crepe with a birthday candle arrived for us to share. The chocolate went perfect with the Triumphator and we almost went for more, but that was it. A happy birthday it was.

The next morning brings us to the train station for a five-hour journey to Ceske Budejovice in the Czech Republic. We will be there for Saturday and Sunday nights. I only wanted one night there, but since we will not arrive until late in the afternoon, we will stay two days to see the sights. I hope it is worth the trip. The main purpose of the stop is to visit the Budvar Brewery. We will pass through the German border into Linz, Austria and then North crossing the border to Czech.

It was a slow, winding, ride with lots of stops. The snow has started up again. I don't mind these train rides, because it gives you a chance to mentally catch up with the trip, and just relax and look out the window.

When we arrive in Budejovice, it is late Saturday afternoon, drizzling, and we notice the streets are empty of people. It was almost a little creepy. The city seems run down, the shop windows are cluttered with signs, but architecturally the city is interesting and pretty. Bohemian King Premysl Otakar II chose the confluence of the large South Bohemian Rivers Vltava and Malse in 1265 to found the city of Ceske Budejovice to strengthen his position of power in South Bohemia. The 16th Century brought extraordinary prosperity to Ceske Budejovice. Considerable profits flowed into the city coffers particularly from silver mining from the surrounding mines as well as beer brewing. The city community used the accumulated money to provide the city with an imposing look. A new city hall building appeared, the city walls were rebuilt and the city council decided to construct a tall clock tower. The horse-drawn tramway, built between 1825 and 1832 as the first on the European Continent, established a link between Ceske Budejovice and the upper Austrian city of Linz. Along with shipping on the Vltava River, Budejovice became a transportation hub.

The direct predecessor of the Budweiser Budvar brewery as a national enterprise was the Czech Share Brewery. It was founded in 1895. During World War II the brewery was under Nazi administration and was nationalized after the War. There has been a decades long trademark battle between Budvar and Anheuser Busch over it's Budweiser brand name. The word Budweiser means, from the Budejovice area. Anheuser Busch used the name some 20 years before the Czech beer came to be named Budweiser.

So, who gets to use the name? Ironically, while we were visiting, Anheuser Busch and Budvar came to an agreement on one item, that Anheuser Busch would distribute Czechvar beer in the USA. Czechvar is the name for Budvar beer sold in the USA. The two companies have not come to any agreement yet as to the international rights. Other countries are making their own decision. Spain has recently recognized Budvar as the true Budweiser beer, but an Italian court has determined that Anheuser Busch has the right to use the Budweiser brand name in Italy.

The two beers do not taste anything alike. I have tasted the Budvar on previous trips, and found it very pleasing. I never thought it as good as the Pilsner Urquell, but nonetheless a fine beer. We are looking forward to a visit to the Budvar Brewery.

We find ourselves in a quiet city on Saturday night. We locate a Staropramen pub with a good menu and a friendly young staff. They help us figure out the menu and we taste most of the Staropramen beer versions. Staropramen is brewed in Prague, and has set up a chain of Husa Pubs to continue the tradition of properly serving their beers. We tried the Granat, which was half dark and half light lager, it was reddish in color, and had a sweet, full flavor. The Lezak was light in color, medium in the hops kick, with a slight bitterness. The Svetly was the pils version, soft in mouth feel. The Cerny was the darkest lager version, just slightly sweet. We were surprised, that a lot of people were sitting at the bar and drinking drinks like orange juice, tea, coffee and water. I thought the Czechs were number one in beer consumption? Maybe we were too early in the evening.

When we wake up on Sunday morning, the sun is shining. We walk along the city walls and take in the architectural sights. The main town square is the largest by actual measurements than anywhere else in Europe. It does seem to be large, with an interesting collection of buildings. Today seems like the perfect day to sit in the Budvar Pivnice, or pub, I just hope it is open. I forgot to check the open hours on the Internet before leaving the USA. The brewery is a two-mile hike North of the square. It's lunchtime, the sky is blue, and we're thirsty.

Since everything else seemed closed and desolate today, all that we could talk about on the 45-minute walk was that Budvar had better be open. Finally, we could see the red neon sign up above a tall, glass office building. As we approach we could see others walking in the front door. Yes! To the side was a little museum and gift shop. We stopped there first and learned that there were no tours today. That's okay, we are off to the pivnice. The pivnice was a cozy, clean room, not too large, with arched vaulted ceilings. There was a small, wooden service bar with brass hardware centered near the front. One large TV was on, but with no sound. It is quiet when we enter and we pick a table directly opposite the bar.

The menu listed food and beer in Czech, Deutsch, and English. Pivo, is the Czech word for beer. The prices were unbelievably low. We could tell we were in for an afternoon of fun. The food was delicious and served in large portions. We tasted all the beer varieties, starting with the simple helles. The Krovzkovany lezak, or helles, light, is a good session beer. It is yellow gold in color, pleasant tasting, something you could drink all day. It was served in a bowl like stein. The regular lezak, or lager, was deeper in color, stiffer head, fuller flavors, and a soft mouth feel with a touch of hops. This beer was served in the regular pint-style glass. The Tmavy lezak, or dark lager, had a hint of bittersweet chocolate, dark brown in color, and a tan head. This was a killer beer, and a half-liter was only $1.20. The Rezane here, meant a beer that was half lager and half dark lager. Once I tasted the dark lager, I was hooked.

This was a tourist stop for sure. We could see small groups of six or eight people come in with their guide and busloads on tour. Nina was taking photos of the bar and bartender and soon got him to smile and pose for a couple of photos, including the two of us behind the bar with him. Soon after, a large group of about forty walked in and the bartender had a surprised look on his face. After watching a few minutes of the chaos, Nina jumped up to the occasion and offered her help in pouring the beers. The bartender loved the idea. He trained her with the first few, then left her alone to pour the next several trays of pivo. It was hilarious to see her concentrate so hard on pouring the beers with the perfect head on them. Her new boss seemed very pleased with his new employee. It was a great photo opportunity. They don't call her the Bavarian Bock Babe for nothing!

After the hard work there was one Budvar variety we still needed to taste, and that was by the bottle. It was the Super Strong Beer, Specialni Pivo, at 7.6%. This fine beer was served in a snifter style glass, with *Bud* etched in large script letters. The beer was 14 carat gold in color, had deep flavors, a little spiciness, and hints of bittersweet chocolate. We kept thinking we were leaving, but we kept sharing another bottle. Great stuff, but we finally slipped away. We were there three or four hours, and our bill for both beer and food came to 499 Czech Koruny. That converts to just $25! Can I live here?

We stopped at one local beer bar on the way back to the hotel. Very, very local. The beers from the tap were still delicious, but we were getting confused with the pricing. The prices were so cheap, it didn't seem right to pay 50 cents, after the conversion, for a beer. We eventually made it back to the Staropramen bar, and there we tasted a special drink. It was a Hoegaarden special. A mojito made with the normal recipe, except replacing the rum with Hoegaarden. Pretty good.

The next morning we are on the train again, headed for three nights in Prague. Even the train here is inexpensive. It's a short ride, but our train has mechanical difficulties and we needed to switch to a bus and then back to the train before reaching Prague. Everyone seemed to just take it in stride. So did we. Luckily, we pack light. We arrive in the main train station and I remember the dark grey gloominess within it's walls. Why this super, historical and architecturally rich city, has such an unwelcoming train station, I will never understand.

Prague is one of the most beautiful European cities and has had many nicknames such as "City of 100 towers", "The Heart of Europe", or "Golden Prague". It was a crossroad, where many merchant, artists and scientists met. It is a 1000 year old, well-preserved city, straddling the Vtlava River. There are seven bridges crossing the river, the most famous being the pedestrian Charles Bridge. The size of the buildings, the different styles of architecture and the shear amount of these beautiful buildings will wow you. It is difficult to take it all in. You find yourself just standing in one spot and looking around you 360 degrees.

Hitler just walked into Prague in 1938 and took over. There is actually some good news in that. Since there was no use of force, the great city was spared destruction, and exists as it always has. As soon as the Germans left in 1945, the Russian Communists then took over. The Czechs revolted in 1968, but were unsuccessful. In 1989, the Czechs tried for independence again, and this time they were successful, along with most of Eastern Europe. Soon after, the Czechs and Slovakians peacefully split Czechoslovakia into two neighboring countries.

There are a few brewpubs I want to visit while we're here. Pilsner Urquell seems to dominate the taps at the pubs here, but first we'll do some sight seeing. Start by walking across the Charles Bridge. Visit the Castle, and St. Vitus church which stands within the castle grounds. The two sites are spectacular. So are the crowds, this city is always crowded. When we stopped for lunch, it was off the main streets in a small bistro type place, Restaurace U Urloje. The sun was shining so we sat outside. They were serving a pilsner that I had never tasted before, Krusovice. The beer was a deep gold color, with a bright white head, that tasted less flowery than the Urquell. Nina and I had a couple of these with lunch. Our waitress was very friendly. I ordered a salad for lunch, an attempt to get some greens in my steady diet of pork, and she emphatically responded with "You can have salad at home! Taste a special plate of the house." She was right. We're on travels for beer, and darn it, I'm eating pork. I'm going to eat the house specialty. So, she talked me into the pork medallions with plum sauce. It was excellent. I'll get my greens another day!

With a slight buzz on from Krusovice, we crossed back to the new town area to search out the famous brew pub U Flecku. From what I have read, U Flecku is a very touristy stop, and that a real beer drinker shouldn't even bother stopping. It just celebrated it's 500th anniversary and I have seen many photos of it. This will be my first visit. We find it easily in an area South of Wencelas Square and close to the river on a winding street.

Inside we find many rooms, maybe eight, with one room open this afternoon. It was built with dark brown woods, and the required large wooden tables. Today the room was about one-third filled with various groups of people, already raising their mugs and shouting "Nazdravi", meaning "cheers" in Czech. Our two mugs of beer are brought to us by a waiter without us having to ask. We have no choices. The beer served is a brown lager. It was slightly sweet with a hint of roastiness, and I can't imagine it having a high percentage of alcohol. It was a good basic dark beer. Another waiter was trying to sell shots of Bucherova, a "Czech Medicine" he called it. Always with a 2 for 1 special. As soon as your beer is two-thirds depleted, the waiter automatically brings you another. Okay, they are quick. Soon, a two-piece band struts in to play with a tuba and an accordion. Boy, they were dressed as tourists would expect, and they could crank out the tunes. They walked the room stopping at each group to ask where they were from. Sweden, New Zealand, England, USA...it was fun to hear the responses. Then the two guys would play three songs from your homeland. They were good and earned frequent tips by having the coins tossed into the tuba. As the coins fell, the musician played musical notes that sounded as if an elephant was laughing through it's trunk. Everyone laughed and everyone tipped!

U Flecku was a tourist machine. About every twenty minutes a new musician would appear, perform, and ask for tips. The waiter was repeatedly attempting to sell the shots of Bucherova, and the over achieving waiter was fast with the beer refills. Even my quick drinking pace was not quick enough for our waiter. One time he tried to drop off a refill and I said no and signaled with my hand. He rolled his eyes at me. Come on, I'm on my sixth beer of the day and its only 4pm! I feel like challenging him, but I remember that this is the Czech Republic, they are #1 in beer consumption. Okay, give me another. Finally, after that last beer, I placed a beer mat over my empty mug to stop the onslaught. When the pushy waiter saw this he seemed impressed and dropped off the bill.

Another brewpub to stop at is U Medvidku which is close to Wencelas Square and was founded in 1466. It's the smallest brewery in Prague. There are several different drinking and eating rooms here. They brew their own beer, plus, they seem to be a Budvar house. I sampled the house brew named Old Gott, which was a semi-dark lager, ruby red in color, with a nice kick of hops, and a malt sweet aftertaste. Very good. It was labeled as a "barique", which I learned from the bartender to mean from old oak barrels. The half-liter mug cost me just 85 cents US.

Also located near the Wencelas Square was Novomestsky Pivovar, "the New Town Brewery". They were the new kid on the block for brewing, with a diverse food menu. This place was large, most of it underground with many interconnected rooms. I think some of the rooms must have been under the building across the street. In the center of the main room is the copper kettle that they actually use to brew the beer. There is no glass partition surrounding it, so you can see, hear, smell, and feel the beer brewing process while you sit at one of the tables. We tasted the Kwasnicovy lezak, which we understood to be an unfiltered lager. It was slightly cloudy with a nice round flavor.

One afternoon we visited the Jewish Quarter of the city. You can purchase a combination ticket and visit six different sites within a few blocks. This area is worth spending a few hours to learn the history of the Jewish people in this city. When you finish the tour, you will most likely be moved and mentally or emotionally exhausted. The weather was changing to rain today.

As we are walking, we notice a street poster for a Brussels type restaurant called Les Moules. We locate it on a map and it is only a couple of blocks away. We decide to head over to it and tickle our taste buds with Belgian ales and mussels. It was a good change of pace for us, to take a break from the pork and lagers. Upon arriving at the place, we notice a bit of a crowd in front. They seem to be filming a movie, set in the 1930's. That sounds like fun, let's go inside and watch.

Walking into Les Moules, it was a typical Belgian style restaurant. Nicely decorated, and at the front door was the beer cooler, filled with Trappist beers. We'll have one of those, one of those and one of those...and bring more moules! We enjoyed our beers, a cheese plate, mussels, and watching the movie production.

Prague is a spectacular city. This was my third visit over ten years, and probably my last. It is a must see at least once in a lifetime. Many people trek into Prague from Austria or Germany for a couple of days. Well worth the effort and the time. Our next stop is towards the West to Pilsen. Recognize the name? Pilsen is the city that all pilsner style beers are named after, because the first pilsner was brewed there in 1842.

The Town of Pilsen was founded at the confluence of four rivers - Radbuza, Mze, Uhlava and Uslava - following a decree issued by the Czech King Wenceslas II, in 1295. From the beginning, the town became a busy trade center located at the crossroads of two important trade routes. They were linking the Czech lands with the German cities of Nuremburg and Regensburg. The historic turning point in the development of Pilsen beer brewing was the year 1838 when thirty-six hectoliters of beer had to be emptied in front of the town hall because of its bad quality. The event had a great influence over the burghers with brewing rights. They agreed to build a modern brewery, which would guarantee the production of a quality Pilsen beer. The builder Martin Stelzer was put in charge of the building, using his knowledge gained when traveling and visiting many foreign breweries. Visiting Bavaria, he met a quirky brewer, Josef Groll. Stelzer arranged for Groll to come to Bohemia and brew beer in Pilsen using the latest method of modern fermentation. Groll accepted the challenge, and on October 5, 1842, he brewed the first golden lager beer, setting an example for lager beer brewing ever since. So, a German brewer in Czech brews the world's first pilsner. However, remember, it was brewed with Czech hops, Czech malt, Czech water, and Czech labor. A trademark for the beer was obtained in 1890.

Of course, we had to go to the brewery for a tour. Urquell has been one of my favorite beers for the longest time. We went to the brewery, which is just a short walk from the main square. Urquell has a good tour that costs only $6 per person, and has some good videos to go with it. We had a pleasant guide that spoke English. First, we learned the brewing process for the umpteenth time, and then we ventured into the underground lagering tunnels. Until the 1990's Urquell was still lagered in giant wooden barrels and stored underground in nine kilometers of cool, dark tunnels. The beer sat here for six to eight weeks. The largest barrel was 37 hectoliters and was about six feet in diameter and ten feet tall. The inside of the barrels was "pitched", or coated, so as not to give the beer any oak flavors.

A highlight of the tour was near the end when we were invited to sample some unfiltered, unpasteurized Urquell from the wooden barrel. Also known as a zwiekel beer. They brew this beer just for the people on the tours and special events. It is no longer sold this way because it is only fresh for about two weeks at its peak. The beer was delicious in its natural state. Our tour was the last of the day for our guide so the usual one, free, small beer, turned into two, large, free beers! That was okay with us. There we stood at 5:30 on a Friday afternoon, in a sandstone tunnel, 30 feet underground, with a temperature of 40 degrees, drinking a zwiekel of the "first pilsner on Earth".

On the grounds of the brewery is a restaurant, Na Splice. It is a large room built from a section of the underground fermentation cellars, "spilka" in Czech. The menu is filled with a large variety of food items. The beer menu is limited to Urquell and it's sister beer Kozel, a dark lager. Urquell use to be brewed in three different variations, the 8, 10, and 12 degrees. A measurement in degrees indicates the amount of sugar present during fermentation and ultimately the percentage of alcohol. Only the twelve-degree is brewed today. We wondered why the beer from the barrel is not available here. Of course, the Urquell tasted great, and I noticed the lack of the floral or perfumy taste that is prominent in the home version, which turns some people off. A half-liter mug cost only $1. We enjoyed lunch before the tour and dinner after the tour.

In the morning, it is time to take the train across the border back to Germany. We both feel like we are going home when arriving in Germany. We are returning to Germany before our flight home to live some more of the beer culture. The Czech language is a little cumbersome for us and we found the pub staffs not very hospitable. Our arrival point in Germany is Nurnberg, just South of Bamberg, in the northern section of Bavaria. Nurnberg was founded nearly 1000 years ago. Despite all the years of history, the city is notoriously known from its role in the 20th Century, when the National Socialists abused the city for their purposes. Adolf Hitler made Nuremberg "City of the Party Rallies", and it was here that the atrocious racial laws were adopted. In 1948, it was here that The International Military Tribunal tried the main war criminals of the Nazi regime of terror, during the "Nuremberg Trials". The city, which was badly damaged by bombs during World War II, today presents itself as a successful blend of a lively past and modern present day life.

Nina and I spent an afternoon here in Nurnberg one Christmas season. We remember a great place for lunch, the Original Nurnberger Rostbratwurstkuche adjacent to the church St. Sebald. They serve those specially spiced little sausages that Nurnberg is famous for. The main cooking grill is located in the center of a small room. They cook about a hundred at a time, over a wood fired grill, and always ready for service. Anyone can easily eat four to six.

On the beer list is Lederer Pils and Tucher Dunkles. The Tuchers, are an old established family of Nurnberg, and have been brewing beers since 1672. The dunkles is smooth, a mild roasty smell and a good bubbly feel on the mouth. Lederer's claim to fame is that their beer was the first freight on German railways in 1836. The pils was good, straw gold color, white foam, with nice hop bitterness. All beers seem to go well with these sausages. Grilled to perfection they seem to have a marjoram spice in them that is pleasing.

There is lots of good sightseeing to do here and near each sight is another good beer stop. We came across Hausbrauerei Altstadthof near the castle on the North end of the city. It was the first new brewery in Bavaria in 25 years when it opened in 1984. There is a biergarten and a small pub area with a few tables and a dozen bar stools. We sat at the bar and noticed several people coming in with empty fliptop bottles and getting refills. The bartender was friendly and explained the beers he had that day. Nina tried the Bock bier. It was 6.6%, red brown in color with some hop zest to it. I went with the Schwarz bier. The first sip tasted of malt, then a bitter sweetness, soft, well rounded at 4.8%. This beer was a winner. The place was getting crowded and we were not going to give up our seats at the bar, especially with this Schwarz bier going down so deliciously. I understand that underneath the pub are 600 year old rock cellars where they lager the beer. We didn't get to see those...there will be a next time.

The next day at lunchtime, we came across a stone staircase on a side street leading down underground. It was named Nassauer Keller. We lowered our heads from hitting the brick ceiling of the staircase and entered a spectacular cellar with gothic vaulted ceilings. The room was filled with low hanging lamp fixtures, wooden benches, candles, and wrought iron decorations. What a beautiful space. The featured beers were from a brewery in Buttenheim, St. Georgen Brau. The beer on the menu that caught my eye was the keller bier. During the whole trip here I have enjoyed the keller beers. This one was a dark, amber gold color, and too easy going down. It was delicious. The second beer was the pilsner and it was delivered as a perfect pour. The bright white head must have stood up two inches above the rim of the fluted glass. The food was delicious. I can't believe how many times I have eaten pork on this trip, and each time it is better than the last. The waitress explained to us that the cellar is 900 years old.

Very close by to Nassauer Keller was Barfusser, and it too was underground. It is a new microbrew pub advertised as a small brewery, big experience. Well small it isn't. It is narrow, maybe 60 feet wide, and about 300 feet long. The brewing kettles are visible. They brew only unfiltered blonde and schwarze beers here. We tasted both, and neither were spectacular, but they were good. This would be a great place for a festival party.

We ate a couple of meals at Der Andechser, in the Deutscher Kaiser Hotel, which features the beers from Kloster Andechs on tap. A large bier hall with vaulted ceilings, wooden floors, good service and good food. We were here too late one evening drinking the doppelbock and talking politics and history with a couple of locals.

Our last day in Germany was planned for Frankfurt. Frankfurt is the financial and commercial capital of Germany. Home to the European Central Bank and the most important stock exchange in the country, it also boasts the best collection of museums, next to Berlin. The city's parks, gardens, original old taverns, elegant shops and vibrant cultural life provide a perfect balance to the ultra-modern architectural style of its high-rise buildings.

The Main River divides the city into North and South. The business district lies north of the river, while the quaint houses and pubs, bars, and restaurants of Sachsenhausen lie to the South. I had only one specific place on our list of pubs to visit in Frankfurt. The real purpose for our stop here was to just get close to the airport for an early train ride of 30 minutes in the morning. We parked our gear at the hotel and set out on the sunny day for a good walk. The destination was the first hausebraueri in Frankfurt. The Zwolf Apostel, or Twelfth Apostle, was opened just 25 years ago. On the first floor it was very small, just a half dozen tables, nicely decorated. Again, the beer list was simply blonde or schwarze. There are simple beer choices here in Germany, but complex beers. They are unfiltered and unpasteurized packed with plenty of flavor. They go down easy with whatever meal you decide to eat.

While eating, the waitress explained to us that the cellar downstairs was finished off and about to open for the evening. We climbed downstairs and found another fantastic cellar. The room featured brick walls, dim lighting, heavy wooden tables and chairs, and a small bar with about six bar stools. Wow, we would love to stay here, but we are finally admitting to being tired. The end of our three-week trip is upon us. Neither of us prefers to fly for ten hours with even the slightest bit of a hangover.

We decide to head back to the hotel with a walk along the Main River. There is a terrific, grassy area and paved path along the river. It seems all the townspeople and tourists were out on this sunny, blue-sky day. We stopped to sit on a bench and watch the activity. We spent an hour watching the sunset and boats float by. It was a moment of relaxation that ended our travels for beer. It had been a torrent pace of chasing down new places, meeting new friends, and drinking new beers. I thought about how lucky the people here were to have this beer culture surround them everyday. How lucky they all were to be able to walk into an ordinary pub and get a great beer along with a great meal whenever they want.

Our three weeks of travel and living the beer culture surely satisfied our thirst and our search for the perfect pubs. We were both satisfied, sitting on that bench in Frankfurt. I'm not sure what Nina was thinking at that moment, but I was thinking about our next trip...

Author's note:
I promised myself before this trip, that upon returning, I would compile a list of the Top 5 beers we tasted during the three weeks. Reading our notes, there are 12 top beers:

Klosterbrau braun or schwarzla in Bamberg
Mahr's Sternen helles in Bamberg
Weihenstephan hefe-weissbier in Freising
Andech's doppelbock in Munich
Ayinger Jahrhundert lager in Aying
Winkler Brau hefe-pils in Legenfield
Weltenburg Baroque Dunkel in Kelheim
Peschl Brau Stephanus heller doppelbock in Passau
Budvar dark lager in Ceske Budejovice
U Medvidku Old Gott dark lager in Prague
Pilsner Urquell unfiltered from the barrel in Pilsen
Hausbraueri Altstadthof schwarze in Nurnberg

I forced myself to compile our Top 5 list. As far as I know, unfortunately, none of these are available in the USA:

Peschl Brau St. Stephanus heller doppelbock in Passau
Weltenburg Baroque Dunkel in Kelheim
Andech's doppelbock in Munich
Klosterbrau braun or schwarzla in Bamberg
Pilsner Urquell unfiltered from the barrel in Pilsen

LAST CALL

Today I am doing the final proof reading of these written adventures. While I am reading, I am reliving all the great moments and wondering what lies ahead. We surely have met some new friends, drank some great beers, and found some inspiring places. Travels for beer is very satisfying, but it also leaves me curious. What other adventures are ahead and what other great beers can be discovered?

I decided to take a break from the proof reading and go for a short walk to the mailbox. To my surprise, inside, was my Stephanus stein that I requested from Peschl Brau in Passau, Germany. According to the return address, it had been shipped from Pennsylvania. Mr. Matthius Peschl has been true to his word and has shipped me the stein, along with several beer mats and a hand written note, while he was traveling in the US.

This was customer service taken to the highest and most cordial level. It reminded me of why I enjoy traveling in Germany, the beer culture. It also prompted me to visit the Peschl website again, where I found an introductory letter from his father, Ernst Peschl, the fifth generation to head the brewery. He states that the family is committed to the customer as well as being committed to brewing high quality beers using old traditional practices. It's evident that they practice what they preach.

What a coincidence that the stein arrives on this the day that I am writing "Last Call" for the book. I honor its arrival by filling it with the best doppelbock from my beer cooler, Ayinger Celebrator. I take a sip. It's just perfect, thank you Mr. Peschl.

I'm dreaming about travels for beer in the future, but I know I need to take care of the present. My business, Stuff Yer Face Restaurant, is in the competent hands of Matthew Poznick. Matt is the General Manager of the restaurant and the bar. It is his hard work, and honesty, that enables me to be away and travel. When we get together for a management session his favorite saying is "We do our best thinking when we're drinking" and so he always keeps a pen and pad handy. We'll be celebrating 30 years for Stuff Yer Face in October of 2007.

I managed to marry a beautiful woman who also likes to travel and taste new beers. Nina, my Bavarian Bock Babe, is easy to travel with, and gets us "behind bars", in a good way. She has tended bar in more cities and countries than anyone I know. The adventures wouldn't be the same without her.

Our recent travels to the different destinations, and especially Bavaria, temporarily quenched my thirst for the beer culture. I am even thirstier now. I think it is time for us to spend two or three months in Bavaria this Fall. I have always wanted to see the harvest of the hops. It will be beer festival season there and we can dodge the hurricanes in Florida by being away.

I'll be sure to keep a good log of the events, because who knows what will happen. If we become part-time residents of Bavaria, I can purchase my first lederhosen and Nina's dirndl. Maybe the title of the next book could be, "Getting fitted for my Lederhosen", or better yet, "Under the Bavarian Chestnut Tree".

For more information on
Stuff Yer Face
go to
www.stuffyerface.com

For more information on
TRAVELS for BEER
go to
www.travelsforbeer.com